A NEW DAY IN CHURCH REVIVALS

BILL V. CATHEY

BROADMAN PRESS
Nashville, Tennessee

To my wife, Rhea

© Copyright 1984 • Broadman Press
All rights reserved
4262-44
ISBN: 0-8054-6244-9
Dewey Decimal Classification: 269.24
Subject Heading: REVIVALS
Library of Congress Catalog Card Number: 83-70645
Printed in the United States of America

Unless otherwise noted, Scripture quotations are from the Revised Standard Version of the Bible, copyrighted 1946, 1952, © 1971, 1973.

Scripture quotations marked (KJV) are from the King James Version of the Bible.

Library of Congress Cataloging in Publication Data
Cathey, Bill V., 1932-
   A new day in church revivals.

  1. Revivals. I. Title.
BV3790.C355 1984   269'.24   83-70645
ISBN 0-8054-6244-9 (pbk.)

Foreword

Last year almost 50,000 revival meetings were conducted in Southern Baptist churches. Unfortunately many of them were more meeting than they were revival. The primary reason for this was inadequate preparation on the part of churches.

One reason for this inadequate preparation in revival meetings is simply a lack of know-how. Many pastors and guest evangelists have little knowledge of how to prepare a church for a revival crusade. It is at this point that the book, *A New Day in Church Revivals* will be of tremendous help.

Bill Cathey, who has worked with revival evangelism in the Division of Evangelism of the Baptist General Convention of Texas for five years, is as competent an authority on this subject as one will find anywhere. In this book he has combined the best of material from many sources to provide an excellent guide for preparation for a local church revival.

There are several books which contain one chapter on the subject of revival evangelism. To my knowledge, however, this is the only book devoted entirely to this subject for sale in book stores.

Every facet of revival preparation is covered in this book. It is filled with usable ideas and plenty of detail on how to employ them. This book is needed. I plan to make use of it in my classes. Pastors and churches will profit a great deal from using it as a manual for revival preparation. I heartily recommend it to you!

Roy J. Fish
Southwestern Baptist Theological
   Seminary
Fort Worth, Texas

Preface

Revival meetings, which are rooted in the New Testament, blossomed in America before it became the United States. The Great Awakening began in 1734 while Jonathan Edwards was preaching a series of sermons on justification by faith. It spread like wildfire under the preaching of evangelists like George Whitefield, John Wesley, Gilbert Tennent, and multitudes of other preachers and pastors whose names never made history.

The revival passed from generation to generation, from north to south, from Congregationalists to Methodists, from Presbyterians to Baptists. The number of churches and church memberships grew rapidly. By the time America became an independent nation, the Christian faith was a way of life. Its influence was felt in forming the Constitution of the United States and the Bill of Rights.

Revival broke out again in the Second Great Awakening of the early 1800s. Camp meetings, where people camped in tents and attended revival services in the open air, played a key roll. Presbyterians, Methodists, and Baptists reaped large results in church memberships.

God used a lawyer turned evangelist, Charles G. Finney, to spark revivals from 1830 until the Civil War.

God took a shoe salesman named D. L. Moody and made a flaming lay evangelist out of him. Annual revival meetings became a part of the church program to reach the unsaved. Camp meetings gave way to revival services in frame tabernacles.

God picked a baseball star, Billy Sunday, to fire the revivals in the early 1900s. Two-week revival meetings were conducted under brush arbors, in community tabernacles, canvas tents, and church buildings. The first week was used to get the church revived and the second week was to win the lost. People joked, "The only time God can give revival is starting the third week in August." That fit the schedule of rural America.

In the 1940s and 1950s, simultaneous revivals under the leadership of C. E. Matthews brought renewed interest to revival meetings. Churches in areas or states—even nationwide—scheduled revivals the same time, pooling their resources. These were years of growth for some denominations.

God raised up Billy Graham to be the leader of revival evangelism during the last half of the twentieth century. His evangelistic association's extensive organization plans set the pattern for revival preparation. His great crusades came at a time when rural America was moving into big cities.

To this day about 75 percent of evangelistic churches schedule one or more revival meetings annually. Trace the growth of Christianity in America, and you will discover that revival meetings have been a key factor in reaching people for Christ and calling the people of God back to him.

In revival preparation workshops, I ask, How many of you were saved either during a revival meeting or as a result of a revival meeting? Usually 50 percent of the people raise their hands. You see, we used to depend on revival meetings for about half of our professions of faith and baptisms. Today many of our churches are not doing that, and it may be one of the reasons we are not reaching more people for Christ.

Some pastors and churches have become disillusioned with revival meetings and have abandoned them. Others have cut back on revival meetings. Some have gone to four-day minirevivals and weekend revivals. Still others have substituted deeper life conferences, Bible conferences, family life conferences, and such. Though all of these are good, when they take the place of revival meetings, the end result is fewer professions of faith.

The answer to the dilemma is not to forsake revival meetings but to alter our approach in preparing for them. That is the purpose of this book, *A New Day in Church Revivals*.

Let me clarify two terms. *Revival meetings* are series of services usually scheduled within a week's time. A *revival* is the movement of God among his people in which spiritual renewal takes place in the lives of Christians and unsaved people are converted. We should do everything we can to make sure that our revival meetings become revivals that last long after the week of services is history. It is my prayer that this book will help us to do exactly that.

BILL V. CATHEY
Division of Evangelism
Baptist General Convention
of Texas

Contents

Section I: The Nuts and Bolts of Planning Church Revival Meetings

1. The Biblical Basis for Revival Meetings   11
2. The Purpose of Revival Meetings   13
3. Principles of Revival Preparation   15
4. Long-Range Preparation for Revival Meetings   19
5. Developing Plans for Revival Meetings   23

Section II: A Cafeteria of Ideas to Use in Planning for Church Revival Meetings

6. Ideas on How to Prepare a Church Spiritually for Revival   31
7. Ideas on How to Reach the Unsaved, Unchurched, and Uninvolved Church Members   37
8. Ideas on How to Build Attendance   44
9. Ideas on How to Publicize Revival Meetings   50
10. Ideas on How to Prepare for Counseling   71
11. Ideas on How to Do Follow-up with New Members   73

Section III: Completed Plan of Preparation for Your Next Revival Meeting

Acknowledgments

I am deeply indebted to many people for their encouragement and assistance:

To my secretary, Loy Beaird, to LaRay Huddelston and Doloris Scherler for typing the manuscript.

To my wife, Rhea, who proofread everything and suggested improvements.

To George Worrell and Gene Jorgenson for critiquing the manuscript.

To Lynda Kokel for the artwork.

To my family at home and my family in the Division of Evangelism for their encouragement and prayers.

To multitudes of pastors and evangelists who developed, used, and refined most of the ideas contained in the book.

To Bobby Sunderland and Richard Harris of the Southern Baptist Home Mission Board for the opportunities to work with them in mass evangelism and to learn from them.

Section I
The Nuts and Bolts of Planning Church Revival Meetings

This is the "how to" section of the book. The first three chapters deal with the biblical basis, purpose, and principles of preparation for revival meetings. The next two chapters present a long-range countdown schedule and the details of composing a set of plans to guide the church in preparing for revival meetings. These guidelines should become a pattern you follow in planning revival meetings year after year.

1

The Biblical Basis for Revival Meetings

The second chapter of Acts sets a pattern for evangelism in New Testament churches which is followed throughout the Book of Acts.

First is prayer. Look at Acts 2:1-4:

When the day of Pentecost had come, they were all together in one place. [Acts 1:14 tells us they were praying.] And suddenly a sound came from heaven like the rush of a mighty wind, and it filled all the house where they were sitting. And there appeared to them tongues as of fire, distributed and resting on each one of them. And they were all filled with the Holy Spirit.

Then notice that they continued to pray day after day: "And they devoted themselves to the apostles' teaching and fellowship, to the breaking of bread and the prayers" (Acts 2:42). Prayer was a priority.

Second is witnessing. Acts 2:4-6 tells us that

they were all filled with the Holy Spirit and began to speak in other tongues [other languages], as the Spirit gave them utterance. Now there were dwelling in Jerusalem Jews, devout men from every nation under heaven. And at this sound the multitude came together, and they were bewildered, because each one heard them speaking in his own language.

They went out from the prayer meeting to witness. Witnessing was a priority in the New Testament church.

Third is gospel preaching. "But Peter, standing with the eleven, lifted up his voice and addressed them" (Acts 2:14). Then he preached the gospel:

Now when they heard this they were cut to the heart, and said to Peter and the rest of the apostles, "Brethren, what shall we do?" And Peter said to them, "Repent, and be baptized every one of you in the name of Jesus Christ for the forgiveness of your sins; and you shall receive the gift of the Holy Spirit. So those who received his word were baptized, and there were added that day about three thousand souls (2:37-38,41).

Gospel preaching was a priority in the New Testament church.

Notice that revival meetings were also a part of their evangelistic strategy: "And day by day, attending the temple together and breaking bread in their homes, they partook of food with glad and generous hearts, praising God and having favor with all the people. And the Lord added to their number day by day those who were being saved." In chapter three, two thousand more converts were added because in Acts 4:4 we are told that the congregation had grown to five thousand.

About this time the Pharisees and scribes and priests began to persecute Christians, but the revival went right on. The people even began to come from miles away to get in on it (Acts 5:16). Acts 5:42 says, "Every day in the temple and at home they did not cease teaching and preaching Jesus as the Christ." They had a revival meeting going.

After Stephen was martyred, the persecution scattered the Christians from Jerusalem, but it didn't stop the revival. It just spread it out. "Therefore they that were scattered abroad went every where preaching the word" (Acts 8:4, KJV).

Even persecutors were converted and joined in the revival. Saul put down his sword, took up preaching, and became Paul, the great missionary (Acts 9:1-2,20-22).

Theological controversy in chapter 15

slowed the effort briefly, but then revivals kept breaking out. "So the churches were strengthened in the faith, and they increased in numbers daily" (Acts 16:5). Then the critics began to complain, saying, "These men . . . have turned the world upside down" (17:6). It would be more accurate to say that God was turning it right side up. Revival meetings were definitely a part of the New Testament plan of evangelism. They should also be a priority in our churches today.

2

The Purpose of Revival Meetings

There are four good reasons churches should have revival meetings.

To Reach the Unsaved and Unchurched

C. E. Autry, a seminary professor of evangelism, taught that "revival time is harvest time."[1] He said that the ground must be broken, the seed planted, proper cultivation and seasoning provided. Then comes harvesttime, revival time.

In past years, revival meetings produced about half of our professions of faith and baptisms. For example, the editor of the *Baptist Standard* reported: "In the March meeting of the Texas Baptist Executive Board, the chairman asked for a show of hands of those who had made their professions of faith in Christ as Saviour in a revival meeting. Almost seventy-five percent raised their hands." He continued, "A similar high percentage would no doubt be the response if the same question was put to most Baptist churches. Baptists have grown up with revival meetings as a method of evangelistic effort. It has been a favorite standby."[2]

Many churches do not schedule revival meetings now as in the past, and this may be one of the major reasons why we are not reaching more people for Christ. For example, I heard a pastor of a large church say that they quit having revival meetings and the number of people being saved declined. So, he said, they were going back to revival meetings out of necessity.

Some churches who have great numbers saved from week to week have proven that revival meetings can add to the harvest. I assisted in revival preparation at the church that led my denomination in baptisms that year. The church averaged about fifteen hundred in Sunday School. More than two hundred professions of faith were registered in the revival week, and over one hundred and seventy of those joined the church by baptism.

Another church which consistently leads its denomination in baptisms relies on a great summer revival meeting to help them win many people for Christ.

Churches need revival meetings to help them reach unsaved and unchurched people in their communities.

To Rereach the Uninvolved Church Members

Most churches would have fantastic revivals if they just rereached their own members who have "dropped out." In fact, most church buildings would not hold the crowd if all the members showed up at one time. So one of the purposes of revival meetings is to reclaim church members who have dropped by the wayside.

Another reason churches need to make an effort to rereach these folk is because some of the best unsaved prospects they have are in the homes of these inactive church members. In some cases there is an unsaved parent, which may be one reason the whole family has become inactive. In many of these families there are unsaved youth and children.

I preached a revival meeting in a church in which a teenager was saved on the first Sunday. We visited her dad the next day at his office. He and his wife were members of the church but seldom attended. During our conversation, he voluntarily confessed that they had been careless about attending church and needed to get started again. The father encouraged us to witness to his older teenage son. We did, and he accepted Christ as his Savior. He and his sister were baptized, and the whole family became active in church. One year later I was visiting with the pastor and asked about this family. He said they remained faithfully involved in church.

There are a lot of families just like that one who need to be reclaimed for our churches. Revival meetings can help us do this.

To Edify Christians

Dr. L. L. Morris, a fellow pastor of mine who became the director of evangelism in our state convention, said, "I would have two revivals a year if no one were saved." He pastored the leading evangelistic congregation in our state. If I understand what he was saying, he meant that church members need revival meetings too.

Bobby Sunderland, who was director of mass evangelism for the Home Mission Board of the Southern Baptist Convention wrote:

> Revival is a retreat with God from the ordinary. Every church should commit itself to attendance and prayer expecting God to do something unusual. Every church needs periods of time when its members can isolate themselves from the cares and pleasures of the world. In this setting they can hear the voice of God clearly. Revival can be a spiritual retreat.[3]

Church members coming night after night to good revival services usually make new commitments and experience a new closeness to God. Our church members need spiritual highs that result in spiritual growth. This should be one of our intentions as we plan revival meetings.

To Strengthen Churches

Good revival meetings will strengthen churches spiritually, numerically, financially, and fellowshipwise. The results should be higher attendance, more converts, larger memberships, bigger offerings, spiritual enthusiasm, and a sweet, loving fellowship.

I recall pastoring a church whose fellowship was wounded like a wing-shot dove. Attendance, offerings, and morale were down, but God used a revival meeting to turn it all around. The church experienced a healing. The fellowship became sweet and loving. People were being saved week after week. Others were joining our church by transfer of membership. Attendance and offerings went up. We experienced a spiritual revival that lived on long after the week became history. A good spiritual revival is just what many similar churches need.

Well-planned, worked-up, prayed-down revival meetings will result in spiritual renewal in your church.

Notes

1. C. E. Autrey, *Basic Evangelism* (Grand Rapids: Zondervan Publishing House, 1959), p. 107.
2. Presnal Wood, "Revival Meeting Evangelism Is Still Needed," *Baptist Standard*, 24 Mar. 1982, p. 6.
3. *Revival Planbook for the Local Church*, Home Mission Board, SBC, p. 9.

3

Principles of Revival Preparation

If you expect to have a successful revival meeting in your church, you must observe some principles. Charles G. Finney, the great evangelist of years ago, said, "It is useless to expect a revival simply by asking for it, without bothering to fulfill the laws which govern spiritual blessings."[1]

Here are some of the laws or principles that govern preparation for revival meetings.

Establish Revival Meetings as a Priority

Schedule the revival week on your calendar well in advance to avoid stuffing it in the cracks of an overloaded calendar. Keep the surrounding dates clear so that revival preparation can be a priority. Then make preparation a priority in your church programming. Throw yourself into it wholeheartedly and get the members behind it with you.

I once assisted a church in revival preparation where the pastor was more excited about selling popcorn with his service club than about having revival in his church. I spent the day training him and his revival committee chairpersons. At lunchtime he took me to his service club because he said he couldn't miss. During the program he talked to his club members about their popcorn sales campaign. He used beautiful charts and posters as visual aids. His enthusiastic presentation impressed me. Yet when we talked about preparing his church for revival, he complained numerous times that it was going to take too much effort. In spite of him, the chairpersons got excited about revival preparation, and they had a good week of services. More people were saved that week and joined their church than had the entire previous year. Yet his complaint to me was, "It took too much time." Thank goodness the committee chairpersons made revival preparation a priority. Just think what could have happened if the pastor had been as excited about it.

Make revival preparation a priority and you will have a much better experience.

Make Adequate Preparation

Most unsuccessful revival meetings are the result of the "Hail Mary" approach to revival preparation. Let me explain. Roger Staubach, former quarterback for the Dallas Cowboys professional football team, made famous the "Hail Mary" pass. In the play-off game with the Minnesota Vikings several years ago, time had almost run out for Dallas with them trailing in the ball game. There was time for one more fourth down desperation play. In the huddle I think that something like this must have taken place. Roger Staubach said to wide receiver Drew Pearson, "You run as fast as you can and as far as you can toward the goal line. I'll throw the ball as hard as I can and as far as I can. Let's hope the two of you get together in the end zone." They broke huddle, went to the line of scrimmage, and snapped the ball. The linemen dug in and blocked. Drew Pearson cut across the field heading toward the end zone, running as fast as he could. Roger Staubach dropped back, cocked his arm, and threw the ball as hard and as far as he could. Luckily, Drew Pearson and the football got together at the goal line about the same time. He miraculously caught the ball, scored, and Dallas won. Roger Staubach called it his "Hail Mary" pass.

He just threw the ball up and prayed and hoped that Drew would catch it and make a touchdown.

Some churches prepare for revival meetings about like that. They schedule a week on the calendar, enlist an evangelistic team, and hope and pray that when the two get together they will have revival. Very seldom does the long bomb, "Hail Mary," desperation pass work in football, though it will once in awhile. So also the "Hail Mary" schedule-and-hope approach to revival preparation will seldom work. Sometimes God gives revival in spite of poor preparation, but usually God gives revival to those who prepare for it. Byron Richardson, an evangelist skilled in revival preparation, says, "You get what you get ready for."

L. R. Scarborough, who first occupied the Chair of Fire at Southwestern Baptist Theological Seminary, said, "Revivals do not go off by spontaneous combustion. If they are to be properly conducted and their results conserved, they must be organized. Half of Billy Sunday's and Dwight L. Moody's success was due to their organization." That is true of Billy Graham. Scarborough also said, "Remember: 'There isn't any easy way to have a good revival. If you would have a great revival in your church, you must make great plans for it.'"[2]

C. E. Matthews, one of our greatest leaders in evangelism, was the mastermind behind the tremendous simultaneous revivals of the 1940s and 1950s. He said that "preparation is seventy percent of the success of the revival crusade."[3] Roy Fish, professor of evangelism at Southwestern Seminary, says that the percentage is even higher than that now.

My professor of evangelism, C. E. Autry, said, "Long and thorough preparation is essential."[4]

Roland Q. Leavell served as superintendent of evangelism for the Home Mission Board of the Southern Baptist Convention, seminary professor of evangelism, and later president of the New Orleans Baptist Theological Seminary. In his textbook he wrote, "A congregation should be reminded that Satan will see to it that revival never comes without an awesome struggle."[5] He stressed the importance of good preparation for revival.

David Ray, a very successful vocational evangelist, said in a letter to me, "The single greatest problem I have with churches is their lack of any real preparation for revival. When churches prepare we usually have a good week. When they don't we usually have a poor week. Please do everything you can to promote preparation. It makes all the difference in the world."

Every once in awhile someone says, "We don't want to do all those things to prepare for our revival meeting. We just want to get out of the way and let God do it." That is about like a preacher saying, "I don't want to do all that sermon preparation. I just want to get up and let God speak through me."

I am convinced that for everything God wants done he has a plan for doing it. Look at the account of creation in the first chapter of the Bible. God had an organized plan that he worked. The plan of redemption is another great example. This plan, which he revealed throughout the Old Testament, began with Adam's and Eve's sin in the Garden. He completed the plan when his Son died on the cross. God has a plan for taking the gospel to all the world. It's contained in the Great Commission (Matt. 28:19-20; Acts 1:8). God has a plan for financing his kingdom's work. It is called tithing. For everything that God wants done, he has a plan to do it.

Likewise, God intends for us to plan and work the plan to prepare for revival in our churches.

Some pastors say, "I just want to get

Principles of Revival Preparation

my church praying for revival. I don't want to do all those other things." I knew one church which did that. Their whole plan of preparation for revival was promotion of prayer. True, prayer is the most important part of revival preparation. This church, however, did nothing to organize the prayer effort. They simply announced it from the pulpit and in the church newsletter. They did not plan prerevival visitation, publicity, or ways to build attendance. They just encouraged people to pray for revival. The week of revival services was a flop.

There are several reasons such services are unsuccessful. Number one, you don't get people praying for revival by just announcing it. You must plan ways to involve people in prayer. If you will give the members a piece of the action in preparing for a revival meeting, they will be more apt to pray for revival. Not many people get serious about praying for the pastor's project unless they are involved in the action.

Certainly, work is no substitute for prayer. Neither is prayer a substitute for work. You must pray and work. It is like the old adage, "We need to pray as if it all depended on God and work as if it all depended on us."

If you want to have a successful revival meeting in your church, you must work up a good set of plans and then work the plans. So principle two is "make adequate preparation for revival meetings." Avoid the schedule-and-hope approach.

Involve Most of the Active Members in Revival Preparation

Planned involvement of the membership is a key to good revival preparation.

One of the reasons for Billy Graham's success in crusades is the huge number of people that his organization gets involved in preparation. If all the committee personnel, all the ushers, all the counselors, all the advisors, and all the choir members attend, they will have a good crowd.

So as you develop your plans, be sure you involve as many of your people as possible. If you will give them a piece of the action in preparation for the revival meeting, they will do better at praying for, supporting, and attending the revival services. They will get more out of it too.

Planned involvement of many members is a must.

Have the Church in a State of Spiritual Revival When the Revival Meeting Begins

In years gone by we scheduled two-week revival meetings. The first week was used to get the church folk revived. The second week was used to win the unsaved. Now we have one week of revival services. By the time the revival week ends, the people are ready for revival but tired of meetings. To offset this feeling, we must make sure our churches are in a state of spiritual revival when the week of services begin. This is best done by thorough, extensive preparation as well as people involvement.

A few years ago I went to preach a revival meeting in a church that made very good preparation. During an all-day prayer meeting on Saturday, spiritual revival broke out. When the singer and I arrived on Sunday, the pastor was on a spiritual mountaintop. When he met us he said, "Welcome aboard. We've got revival under way." And they did. It wasn't just a "meetin' " either. We experienced some things that only God can do. One of the good things about a revival meeting like this is that the revival lasts long after the week of services is history. Oftentimes, if your revival comes with the evangelistic team, the momentum leaves with them. When the week is finished, the revival is over. But if your church is in a state of spiritual revival when the week begins, it will live on long after the evangelistic team has gone home.

Church Revival Preparation

This ought to be a goal for all revival preparation: to have the church in a state of spiritual revival when the revival meeting begins.

Apply these principles of revival preparation and your church will have a better experience. Violate these laws of planning and you will probably be disappointed with your revival meeting. Good preparation is worth the effort.

Notes

1. Roland Q. Leavell, *Evangelism: Christ's Imperative Commission* (Nashville: Broadman Press, Revised 1979), p. 146.
2. L. F. Scarborough, *With Christ After the Lost* (Nashville: Broadman Press, 1952), pp. 119, 120.
3. C. E. Matthews, *The Southern Baptist Program of Evangelism* (Nashville: Convention Press, 1956), p. 40.
4. C. E. Autry, *Basic Evangelism* (Grand Rapids: Zondervan Publishing House, 1959), p. 107.
5. Roland Q. Leavell, *Evangelism: Christ's Imperative Commission* (Nashville: Broadman Press, Revised 1979), p. 145.

4

Long-Range Preparation for Revival Meetings

This chapter contains an advance schedule of preparation for church revival meetings.

Calendar Revival Meetings One to Two Years in Advance

There are three reasons to calendar revival meetings in advance: (1) to make revival meetings the priority for a specific period of time on the calendar, (2) to allow adequate time to secure an evangelistic team, and (3) to budget for revival meetings at annual budget planning time.

Let's pursue the first reason a little further here. The other two will be discussed later.

Long-range scheduling is necessary to avoid selecting dates too close to other big church events. Try to save four weeks before and two weeks after the revival meeting for preparation and follow-up. That doesn't mean that everything else stops during this time. It simply means giving some breathing room on the calendar to the revival meeting.

Prayerfully and Carefully Select the Evangelistic Team One to Three Years in Advance

Pastors, don't just ask your buddies or fathers in the ministry to preach your revival meetings. Prayerfully consider and select a person you believe can best help you and your church experience lasting revival.

Don't be like a pastor friend I recall from college days. He said, "I don't ever get an evangelist who can preach better than I can." And do you know what? About two years later he asked me to preach a revival meeting in his church. To say the least, my ego was bruised. I accepted his invitation anyway. On Tuesday when the revival meeting broke loose, he cut loose from me as well. When the people responded to my preaching, he became jealous. But listen, we should be pleased when our folk respond in a positive and enthusiastic way to the evangelistic team we have invited. The better my people liked the evangelist I selected, the better I liked it too.

Get the best evangelistic preacher and singer you can. To do this, you must enlist them a year or more in advance. Preachers in some churches say, "The best revival preachers won't come to little churches like mine." Well, maybe there are a few big shots who think it is beneath their dignity to preach in smaller churches. Usually, however, the reason the bigger churches get these preachers is because they ask well in advance. Most preachers are willing to preach wherever they feel God wants them, regardless of the size of the church. The biggest factor in getting these choice preachers for revival meetings is asking them far enough in advance that they will still have openings in their schedules. This is one of the secrets of securing the best evangelistic help.

If the pastor moves to another church before the revival date, then he asks the evangelistic team to keep the dates with him in his new church. Besides, it is usually best for the pastor who follows if he has the opportunity to select an evangelistic team of his own choosing. Most evangelists would prefer this too.

Avoid asking people on the spur of the moment to preach or lead the singing for your revival meeting. Since I am on the evangelism staff of my state convention, I preach all over the state. Many times after I have spoken, someone will ask me to preach a revival meeting for him. I make it a habit never to accept an invitation until both of us have time to pray about it. I tell him, "If you really want me to come to your church, please pray about it and write me a letter with one or two options on dates." Many times I never receive the correspondence. The pastor simply asked me on the spur of the moment before he had time to pray and think through his invitation.

To avoid misunderstandings, establish some mutual understandings with your evangelistic team.

Dates: Be sure you have agreed on the same dates and the same year. I have known evangelists to have one date on their calendar and the church another, some even different years. If you enlist evangelists over one year in advance, then reconfirm the dates in correspondence each year.

Finances: Share the church policies regarding revival finances with the evangelists. If there are differences of opinions, they need to be settled before the invitation is confirmed.

Lodging: Talk to the team about where they will be staying during the revival week. Find out their preferences about staying in a home or motel. Most evangelists prefer motels. I have stayed in homes where I was assigned a bedroom without a desk or chair or adequate lighting. I have stayed in homes where the lady of the house and I were the only ones at home during the day. I have also stayed in homes where I had very little privacy to pray and study because of small children. For these reasons and others, I prefer a motel room. Some evangelists may prefer homes. Have an agreement on this.

Some other things that need to be settled before the evangelistic team arrives are mealtimes, schedule of services, and selling of records. Some evangelists prefer to eat after the services. Be sure they know about morning or noon services if you have these. If your church has a policy about selling records, be sure your singer knows this before he starts hauling his records into your auditorium.

You may want to discuss other things, such as the giving of the invitations, length of services, and whether the evangelist's wife is going to accompany him.

The question is often asked, "Is it best to have the evangelistic team present for the first or last Sunday?" There are pros and cons either way. Usually it is best to have the team present for the first Sunday morning to expose them to the largest crowd at the beginning of the revival meeting. If the people hear them on the first Sunday, then it should create a desire to hear them throughout the week. In the majority of churches, it would be best to begin on Sunday with the team and conclude with them on Friday. With most congregations, it is best not to have Saturday night services. Thus, the evangelistic team will have ample time to travel back to their own churches or to their next revival meeting on Saturday. Then the pastor and minister of music will conduct the service on the last Sunday. Hopefully, the service that morning will be the biggest and best of the whole week.

On the last Sunday evening of a good revival meeting, it might be best to have a testimonial service. Let the people have an opportunity to share decisions they have made, what the revival has meant to them. Sometimes this will break out into the best revival service of the whole week. The pastor should have a sermon ready to preach, but it just might be that the people will take all the time sharing

Long-Range Preparation for Revival Meetings

testimonies. Some such services have lasted for hours with the pastor only presiding.

Budget for Revival Meetings Expenses in the Annual Budget

When it comes time to formulate the annual church budget, present to the budget committee a detailed request of funds for your revival meetings. Following is a form entitled "Budgeting for Revival Meetings." Give the budget committee a request form like this so they will know exactly why you need the funds.

BUDGETING FOR REVIVAL MEETINGS
Travel Expenses for Evangelists $ _____
   Preacher: _____ (mi.) × _____ ¢ (per mile) = $ _____
      or plane fare $ _____
   Singer: _____ (mi.) × _____ ¢ (per mile) = $ _____
      or plane fare $ _____
Lodging for Evangelists ...... $ _____
   $ _____ (per night) × _____ (no. of nights) × 2
   (preacher and singer)
Meals for Evangelists .... $ _____
   $ _____ (per day) × _____ (no. of days) × 2
   (preacher and singer)
Promotion and Publicity ...... $ _____
   (materials, printing, postage, etc.)
Miscellaneous (guest personalities, church meals, etc.) .... $ _____
TOTAL .... $ _____

Locate Prospects Six Months Before Revival Meeting

The single biggest reason why more unsaved people don't attend revival meetings is inadequate prospect files. In one of my revival plans, which hundreds of churches in our state have used, there is a good plan to enlist people to visit. Too many times, however, churches have more people willing to visit than they have prospect assignments.

In chapter 7 numerous ideas are offered on how to locate prospects.

Begin a Plan of Cultivation of Unsaved Prospects Four Months Before the Revival Week

The pastor, church staff, and active members need to have or be assigned a number of unsaved and unchurched families to cultivate. You might want to promote a "Ten Most Wanted List" of persons who are unsaved and unchurched. Those joining in this effort would pray daily for the persons on their list. They would maintain contact through visits, phone calls, social events, and helping in times of need. Their goal is to cultivate friendship and trust so that these persons will listen to them, attend church with them, and respond to God's invitation to become his children. This is a must in reaching most adults.

The pastor and church staff should lead out in this. Each staff member needs about fifteen to twenty-five people whom they are cultivating for Christ and his church. If just the church staff does this, many people will be saved. When the evangelistic team arrives, they should join the staff in visiting these people.

Let me share a good example. When a pastor picked me up at the airport, he showed me an index card with about fifteen or sixteen names on one side. He said, "I've been working with these unsaved people, and I want us to visit every one of them and share the gospel. If we get to all of these, I have more." He showed me the other side of the card with more names. During the week, he made appointments with each of these people. We visited three or more each afternoon starting about four o'clock. When I presented the gospel to these people he had been cultivating, almost all of them were won to Christ in their homes. They came to the services and made professions of faith. Every time I stood to preach, I knew someone was coming for salvation during the invitation. Many people were saved during the week, and the reason was the pastor's cultivation of unsaved prospects. This is the way it ought to be done.

Secure or Develop a Plan of Preparation at Least Three Months Before the Revival Week

Make a file for revival preparation. Collect as many plans and ideas as possible. When you hear of a church that had a good revival meeting, get ideas from them. If possible, secure a copy of the plans they used. Collect revival plan books from evangelists. Build up a big file of preparation ideas. Then about three months before your revival week, secure or develop a set of preparation plans. The next chapter deals with this in detail. In the last section of this book is a completed plan of revival preparation which you can use to plan for your next revival meeting.

Your evangelist may provide or suggest revival preparation plans. If he has a plan, do your best to follow it as closely as possible.

It's an old saying but it is true, "If you want to have a good revival, you must plan and then work the plan."

Enlist and Train Revival Committee Chairpersons and Begin Countdown Preparation Two Months Before Revival Week

After you have secured or developed a set of preparation plans, enlist capable people to be chairpersons. Seven to eight weeks before the revival meeting, spend some time with each chairperson reviewing instructions and responsibilities.

Do an Evaluation After the Revival Week

After the revival week has ended, set aside a time to evaluate all the plans used in preparation for the revival. Make notes on things that work well and should be repeated. Also make notes on areas that could be improved and used again. Perhaps there will be some things you will want to note as bad ideas and should be scrapped. Always determine what you can do to make sure that your next revival meeting is even better than the last one.

5

Developing Plans for Revival Meetings

You need a set of plans that will help your church to prepare for a successful, spiritual revival. This chapter presents some guidelines for preparing such plans. The completed plan in the last section of the book is an example of this kind of planning.

Set Some Goals

First, decide on what you want to accomplish in your planning, then set goals. For example, in one of my revival plan books I suggest these goals for the pastor and revival steering committee:
1. Have the church in a state of spiritual revival when the revival week begins.
2. Involve as many people as possible in revival preparation.
3. Average as many people in the evening revival services as you average in Sunday School attendance.
4. Baptize, as a result of the revival, at least ten persons for every one hundred people in average Sunday School attendance.

Goals need to be measurable. They should be challenging but reachable. They should serve to guide you in your planning. To have goals without action plans is like building an upstairs in a house without the stairsteps. So let's discuss the plans.

Decide on Specific Plans

Here are some guidelines you can use each time you prepare plans for revival meetings.

1. **Decide on Ideas to Help Prepare the Church Spiritually for Revival.**

For example, in the completed plan, these ideas were chosen:
   (1) Lead members to pray daily for revival;
   (2) Have a special prayer for revival during the morning and evening services two Sundays before the revival week;
   (3) Conduct in-church cottage prayer meetings during the midweek services one or two Wednesdays before the revival week;
   (4) Encourage leaders of church organizations to have prayer for revival in all their meetings (Sunday School, deacons' meetings, etc.);

In chapter 6 many good spiritual preparation ideas will be presented that can be used in planning revival meetings for years.

Remember the goal is to have the church in a state of spiritual revival when the meeting begins.

2. **Decide on Plans to Reach the Unsaved, Unchurched, and Uninvolved Church Members.**

Two things are needed for this, pre-revival visitation and a telephone campaign.
   (1) Visitation. For every revival meeting, you need plans to enlist church members to visit both prospects and inactive members. In most of my plans, I suggest that we visit less active members during week two before the revival meeting. During week one, we concentrate on visiting unsaved and unchurched prospects.

It would also be a good idea to begin cultivative witnessing plans at least three months or more before the revival week. Enlist soul-winners and help them to prepare prayer lists of unsaved persons they are going to try to reach by the end of the revival week.

The pastor himself should have fifteen or twenty persons that he is cultivating to visit with the evangelist during the revival week. This will result in many professions of faith if the pastor will work at it.

(2) Telephone campaign. In every revival meeting, you need to organize a telephone crew to call all church members and prospects. In smaller communities, call every residence listed in the telephone book. Numerous suggestions on how to organize revival visitation and telephone campaigns will be discussed in chapter 7.

3. Decide on Ways to Build Attendance.

It is a proven fact that specific plans are needed to build attendance at every revival service, especially week nights. For example, in the completed plan this schedule is used:

Monday:	Sunday School Rally Night
Tuesday:	Youth Joy Explosion—one hour before service
Wednesday:	Men and Women's Night
Thursday:	Children's Corny Dog Supper—one hour before service
Friday:	Family Night
Saturday:	Music Night
Sunday:	High Attendance in Sunday School

In chapter 8 a variety of ideas to build attendance will be presented.

Remember, the goal is to average as many people in evening services as you average in Sunday School. Plan carefully and specifically if you want to reach the goal.

4. Decide on Ideas to Publicize the Revival Meeting.

You need "inside" publicity which is aimed specifically at the church membership. You also need "outside" publicity to advertise the revival meeting to the whole community.

Consider these ideas:
(1) Posters
(2) Visitation leaflets
(3) Bulletin covers or inserts
(4) Promotion in church newsletters
(5) Announcements in Sunday bulletins
(6) Letters to members and prospects
(7) Advertisement in newspapers
(8) News releases in newspapers
(9) Large sign in churchyard
(10) Signs in members' yards
(11) Radio and television spots
(12) Community announcements on radio and television
(13) Billboards
(14) Door-to-door circulars
(15) Banners across main streets
(16) Display of revival theme in church auditorium

Many detailed plans to publicize revival meetings will be discussed in chapter 9.

5. Decide on Ways to Enlist Revival Choir.

Music plays an important part in revival meetings. Make it a goal to have the choir loft filled for each revival service. Plan a sign-up campaign. Don't leave it to chance. Consider asking older youth to sing in the revival choir.

6. Decide on Plans to Assist Those Who Make Public Decisions During Invitations.

This will involve enlisting and training counselors. If you expect to have several people coming during the public invitations at revival services, counselors are a must. There is a principle that says, "When the line starts forming to talk to the pastor during invitations, the people

Developing Plans for Revival Meetings

stop coming." So use counselors. When inquirers come forward, the pastor, and maybe staff members, should first receive them. Shortly thereafter a counselor should be called to assist the inquirer. Chapter 10 deals with this matter in detail.

7. Decide on Ways to Follow Up with New Members.

The task of reaching people for Christ is not completed when they join the church. They must be assisted to become active in the church and to grow as Christians. Too many churches fail at this point, so be sure to have a good follow-up plan to assist those who join your church during revival meetings.

The pastor or a follow-up counselor should visit new converts immediately after their public professions of faith. Counselors should review the plan of salvation with the new converts to be sure that they are saved. They should explain the meaning of baptism and plan the baptism service with the candidates.

Within the week, Sunday School teachers should contact new members who are prospects for their classes. The very best plan of follow-up for a new member is a Bible teaching, caring, loving Sunday School class.

New member orientation classes are helpful. There are also many good discipleship plans available to help new Christians grow spiritually.

In chapter 11 numerous ideas and details on how to follow up with new members will be presented.

Decide on Committees Needed

Use these committees in planning every revival meeting: Prayer Committee, responsible for spiritual preparation; Visitation Committee, responsible for pre-revival visitation; Telephone Committee, responsible for telephone campaign; Publicity Committee, responsible for revival advertisement; Music Committee, responsible for enlisting revival choir; Counselor Committee, responsible for counseling inquirers.

Then you need committees to be responsible for building attendance. For example, in the completed plan in the last section, these committees are suggested: Sunday School Committee, responsible for Sunday School Rally Night; Youth Committee, responsible for Youth Joy Explosion on Tuesday; Adult Committee, responsible for Men and Women's Night on Wednesday; Children's Committee, responsible for Corny Dog Supper on Thursday; Contact Committee, doubles as Telephone Committee and is responsible for Family Night on Friday; Music Committee, responsible also for Music Night on Saturday.

Prepare Instructions and Countdown Calendars for Chairpersons

Instructions should communicate to each chairperson exactly what to do, how to do it, and when to do it. Experience proves that if chairpersons have these handles on their responsibilities, they will do good jobs.

Apply the "KIS" principle, that is "Keep It Simple."

On pages 27 and 28 are samples of instructions and countdown calendars.

As you prepare the countdown calendars for chairpersons, keep a record of all entries on a big master countdown calendar. Make brief notations of each chairperson's instructions on the big calendar with name of committee responsible. For example, on week number one of the children's chairperson countdown calendar the instructions might be to "Mail letter and tickets to children who are Sunday School members and prospects." On week number one of the master countdown calendar note: "Mail letter to children—Children's Chp."

This will keep you from overloading any area of the revival calendar. It will also help you to know who is supposed to be doing what and when. This master countdown calendar can be used as a checklist at steering committee meetings, which will be discussed soon.

Enlist and Train Committee Chairpersons

Enlist chairpersons nine to ten weeks before the revival meeting. Train them seven to eight weeks before the revival week.

1. Enlist Chairpersons.

Select the best persons you have to chair committees: staff or lay members.

Use as many of the leaders of the organizational structure in your church as possible. For example, the Sunday School Committee chairperson should be the Sunday School director. His committee should be Sunday School Department directors or class teachers. The Music Committee should be chaired by the choir director or choir president. Section leaders or choir officers would be on the committee. The Children's Committee chairperson ought to be a Sunday School worker with children. Other children's workers should serve on the committee.

When you use your church leadership like this, continuity is added. Plus it is a natural and easy way to enlist the most qualified people to serve as chairperson and committee members.

2. Train Chairpersons.

Seven to eight weeks before the revival meeting, spend about thirty minutes with each chairperson. The best way to do this is simply read through the instructions with the chairperson. Fill in dates on the appropriate calendar, make explanations and answer questions. The worst way to do this is to give the chairperson instructions and tell him to do what it says.

If you make sure that all chairpersons know exactly what to do, how to do it and when to do it, they will usually do good jobs.

Bring all the committee chairpersons together soon after they have all been trained individually. Do a brief overview of the total plans so that each chairperson can see the whole plan and how his or her part relates to it. This will be an exciting meeting.

Schedule Steering Committee Meetings

Chairpersons of the various committees make up the steering committee with the pastor usually serving as general chairperson. Meet weekly starting three to four weeks before the revival week. Sunday night before or after the service is a good time. Most chairpersons will already be at church, and it saves being out another night.

At steering committee meetings, each chairperson gives a progress report. It is also a good idea to have a master countdown calendar which was discussed earlier in this chapter. At each meeting, review the work each chairperson is supposed to have done by that time. Then review what is supposed to be done before the next meeting. Offer to assist those behind schedule.

Oftentimes decisions will be made at steering committee meetings. Always there should be a time of prayer.

Special Note

In the next section is a truckload of ideas and details to do the things discussed in this chapter.

A plan put together exactly as instructed in this chapter is contained in the last section of this book. Use it to get ready for your next revival meeting. After that, put together your own plans. Sometimes God gives revival in spite of poor preparation, but God usually gives revival to those who prepare for it. Sure, it takes a lot of time and hard work, but the end result will be well worth the effort.

1. Keep one copy in the book.
2. Give one copy to chairmen.

Planning for Revival

Contact Chairman

This committee is responsible for two things: (1) telephoning all the church families and prospects before the revival week; (2) helping build the attendance for Family Night on Friday by a written invitation and a second telephone call to all the church families and prospects.

Ask the church secretary, minister of education or pastor to help you determine the number of church families as well as the number of prospective families. If only one family member belongs to the church, consider this a family. Remember, the rest of the family are prospects.

Church families   _____ (number)

Prospective families   _____ (number)

TOTAL families to contact   _____

On Family Night you might want to have special recognition for the family with the most relatives present and/or let families introduce relatives who are guests. For example, ask children to introduce grandparents.

Instructions for Reproducing Memo and Invitation Cards

On a separate page in the book you have two pieces of art work, "Memo to Revival Contact Crew" and "Family Night at the Revival" invitation cards. Be sure you have these. (Check with the General Chairman.)

The memo is ready to reproduce as is or you may want to rewrite it. Put your name beside "Contact Chairman." To reproduce the invitation cards, fill in the information needed. Make copies, and cut cards apart. These must be on card stock for mailing. Ask the Revival Secretary to help with this.

If there is no Revival Secretary, type or handwrite the information on cards. To reproduce, you might take them to a quick print shop, or have copies made on a copy machine. Many banks, schools, or other churches have copy machines and may help you with this. One way or another, you can do it. <u>Ask the pastor to help.</u>

Contact Chairman Countdown Calendar

Week	Sunday	Monday	Tuesday	Wednesday	Thursday	Friday	Saturday
VI	Enlist committee. If you have less than 150 families (members and prospects) to contact, your Contact Crew will be your committee. If you have more than 150 families (members and prospects) to contact, you need one committee member for every 150 families to be contacted. Enlist one or two from each adult Sunday School department.						
V							
IV	Enlist Contact Crew. Each committee member enlists 10 people from his/her Adult Sunday School department to serve on the Contact Crew. Each Contact Crew member will be responsible for contacting 15 families (members and prospects). In churches with less than 150 families, enlist one crew member for each 15 families to be contacted.						
III	STEERING COMMITTEE MEETING: Be prepared to give progress report.	Prepare assignments. Put 15 names of church families and prospects to be contacted on each page. Give each caller an equal number of church families and prospective families to call. Then assign each page of 15 families to be contacted to a Contact Crew member.					
II	STEERING COMMITTEE MEETING: Be prepared to give progress report.	Ask the secretary to help reproduce the memo, with instructions and the invitation cards (see samples). The committee is to address, stuff, stamp, and mail the memo by Friday. (See instructions for reproducing these materials on the front page of these instructions.) Be sure to send a page about the evangelistic team and revival events with the memo; also include a list of families and telephone numbers.					
I	STEERING COMMITTEE MEETING: Be prepared to give progress report.	Contact committee and crew members address invitations to church and prospective families. (Many churches have addressing machines and can be used for members. Ask secretary about this.) Mail these on Monday of the revival week. Don't mail too early.			Contact Crew make first telephone calls to all those assigned to them.		
REVIVAL	Call all Contact Crew and remind to make second calls. Ask the pastor to promote Family Night during each revival service.	Mail Invitations	Contact crew make second telephone calls to those assigned to them.			FAMILY NIGHT	

Fill in revival dates then back up and fill in the other dates on the calendar. You will have a tailor-made countdown calendar for your committee.

Section II
A Cafeteria of Ideas to Use in Planning for Church Revival Meetings

This section contains numerous ideas you can use in developing plans for revival meetings. Please be aware that you cannot use all the ideas in each chapter in one revival meeting any more than you can eat in one meal everything that a cafeteria serves. There are enough ideas to help you plan many revival meetings with variety. Hopefully, the ideas will spark your imagination to be creative.

The ideas used in the completed plan in Section III of this book come from the ideas suggested in this section.

6

Ideas on How to Prepare a Church Spiritually for Revival

Getting Members Committed to Pray for Revival

In preparation for every revival meeting, you need to set aside a time to challenge the people to pray for revival. Do this during one of the Sunday worship services or maybe during the midweek service two or three weeks before the revival meeting.

Prepare commitment and reminder cards like those on page 33. During the service give everyone present a "Prayer Commitment Card" to sign and return. You may want them to keep the cards as a reminder if you don't use the small reminder cards. Also give each family a "Family Prayer for Revival" folder to put on the table where they eat to remind them to pray for revival when they say the blessing.

Consider preaching on prayer or spiritual preparation for revival during the sermon time.

Small Group Prayer Meetings

1. In-Church Cottage Prayer Meetings During Midweek Service

Do this for one to two Wednesdays before the revival week. Meet together for a brief word from the pastor then break up into small groups, six to eight people in each. Designate someone to be the leader of each group. Give the leaders a suggested guide to follow. (Sample guides are given later in this chapter.)

2. Cottage Prayer Fellowships After Sunday Evening Services

Scheduling these on Sunday night after the service avoids taking members away from home another night. This is especially important if other nights are used for prerevival visitation.

Schedule these for two or three Sundays before the revival week. Meet in homes of members or at church. If you have these in the church buildings, follow procedures suggested for In-Church Cottage Prayer Meetings. If you meet in homes, select families in various areas of the community to be hosts. Hosts will provide light refreshments. Also select leaders for the groups and give them a suggested guide to follow. Leaders and hosts are responsible for enlisting people in their area to attend with them.

Youth might have their own prayer fellowship. Provide child care for grade school and preschool children.

Before the benediction in the Sunday evening service, the pastor needs to announce these prayer meetings, introduce hosts and leaders, and encourage members to attend one of the prayer fellowships.

3. Cottage Prayer Meetings in Homes

Schedule these for one to two weeks before the revival meeting, one or two nights each week. There is one big disadvantage to these cottage prayer meetings. If you schedule prerevival visitation the two weeks before the revival meeting as well as cottage prayer meetings, you are asking people to be away from home too many nights. They will be "met out" before the revival services ever start.

Enlist families to host cottage prayer meetings in their homes. They will provide light refreshments. Leaders need to be enlisted and given a suggested guide to follow. Both hosts and leaders are responsible for enlisting people to attend with them.

Publish dates, locations, hosts and leaders in Sunday bulletins and weekly newsletters. The pastor should promote this from the pulpit.

4. "Prayertations"—Prayer and Visitation Combination

Organize this much like the suggestions for home cottage prayer meetings. The leader will also be provided visitation assignment cards to give to the people.

Don't serve refreshments for this will use up valuable time. Take about thirty minutes for prayer. Then make visitation assignments and spend about forty-five minutes visiting.

Prayer Meetings on Saturday Before Revival Week

Use some variation of this before every revival meeting.

1. Launch Prayer Meeting—To Launch the Revival

Schedule it early in the evening at the church. If the evangelistic team can be present, ask them to sing and speak briefly. Then divide into small groups.

You might ask Sunday School Department directors or class teachers to be responsible for the attendance of their departments and classes. Small groups would then be departments or classes with directors and teachers in charge.

Provide child care for grade school and preschool children.

2. Home Cottage Prayer Meetings

Use suggestions as outlined earlier in the chapter. The Saturday before the revival week is an excellent time for Cottage Prayer Meetings.

3. Men's Prayer Breakfasts, Women's Prayer Coffees, and Youth Prayer Fellowships

Enlist a men's prayer captain and a women's prayer captain for this responsibility. If there is a Youth committee, ask them to be responsible for Youth Prayer Fellowship. Otherwise enlist an adult worker with youth to be the youth prayer captain.

At the Prayer Breakfasts and Coffees, people might participate as one large group or have the persons at each table to be a small prayer group.

The Youth Prayer Fellowship should be a combination of prayer meeting and recreation. Serve light refreshments.

These might be scheduled for two or more Saturdays prior to the revival week. Check with those planning to attend to see if child care needs to be provided.

4. All-Day Prayer Meeting

It can be an All-Night Prayer Meeting but consider safety factors.

The length of the prayer meeting will depend on the size of the church. Enlist a prayer captain from each Adult and Youth Sunday School Department. Assign captains one hour apiece. They are responsible for signing up two different groups to join them in prayer. Each group will have thirty minutes. In smaller churches enlist a prayer captain from each adult and youth class and assign them only half an hour. If you have three adult departments and two youth departments, then your prayer meeting will be five hours in length. In smaller churches you might call it a Two-Hour Prayer Meeting or a Three-Hour Prayer Meeting, depending on the number of classes.

Meet in a specially arranged room or at the altar in the auditorium.

Make an "All-Day Prayer Meeting" chart and display it in a prominent place. Make it big. For each hour put the time, prayer captain's name, department (or class), and the time for each prayer group

Prayer Commitment Card

for Revival _____(dates)

_____ Yes, I will pray daily for our revival. I will set aside a time each day at approximately _____ (time of day).

_____ Yes, my family and I will pray for our revival daily.

Signed _____

Church Revival

Remember to Pray Daily for Our

_____ (dates)

Please put this card in a place to remind you to pray for our revival.

(Fill in the dates and names in blanks and reproduce.)

Remember to Pray for Revival

Fold along dotted line and set up on meal table

evangelist _____   singer _____

dates _____

Family Prayer for Revival

Family Prayer for Revival

dates _____

evangelist _____   singer _____

Remember to Pray for Revival

Fold along dotted line and set up on meal table

Ideas on How to Prepare a Church Spiritually for Revival

with spaces to write in names. Here is a sample hour:

9:00 Prayer Captain: John Doe
     Department: Adult II
    9:00 _____
          _____
    9:30 _____
          _____

Prayer captains need to enlist six people or more for each thirty minutes. On Friday evening or Saturday morning before the prayer meeting, captains are to call all those they signed up and remind them to be present. Some people will forget if not reminded. Provide each prayer captain with a suggested prayer guide. (Samples are given later in this chapter)

5. Prayer Vigil

Start at 6:00 AM on Saturday and end at 6:00 AM on Sunday. One person or couple will be enlisted for each thirty minutes. Those scheduled to pray could come to the church or schedule this time at home. Each person telephones the person or persons with the next thirty minutes just before his prayer time starts. This reminder helps to keep the chain from being broken. Smaller churches schedule twelve hours or less.

Prayer Guides for Small Group Prayer Meetings

Provide leaders of prayer groups a guide like these.

Sample 1
(1) Read Luke 6:12-13. Before big events, Jesus spent much time in prayer.
(2) Read Psalm 139:23-24 and 1 John 1:9. Have silent time for self-examination and confession to God.
(3) Pray for the evangelistic team, pastor, and staff.
(4) Ask for prayer requests, and pray for them one at a time as requests are made.
(5) Have a time of prayer when members pray for courage to witness during the revival meeting.
(6) Close with a time of silent prayer when members commit themselves to God and the revival effort.

Sample 2
(1) First read 2 Chronicles 7:14. Discuss briefly.
(2) Pray for the church to experience spiritual revival, starting with us.
(3) Have silent prayer when members examine themselves and confess their sins to God.
(4) Pray for the evangelistic team by name.
(5) Ask for prayer requests and have someone to voice a short prayer for each individual request. Pray especially for unsaved friends and neighbors.

Special Prayer During Church Services

1. Special Prayer for Revival During Worship Services

During the morning and evening worship services two Sundays before the revival week, schedule a time in the order of service for "Special Prayer for Revival." Enlist dedicated members who simply lead in public prayer for revival. They might also share short conversion testimonies.

2. Special prayer in Sunday School Departments and Classes

Ask department directors and class teachers to have a special prayer for revival each Sunday two weeks or more before the revival meeting. You might put up special prayer posters in class rooms or write a note on the chalkboard reminding them to pray for revival.

3. Special Prayer in All Meetings

Ask leaders of all church organizations and committees to have special prayer for revival every time they meet, starting about one month before the revival week.

Prayer Partners

This is two people who agree to pray for revival at a specific time each day. They may or may not meet together. The telephone might be used for this.

Begin signing up people for this about three weeks before the revival meeting. Use a commitment card that has this information on it:

"Realizing the importance of prayer, I will select a prayer partner to join me at a set time to pray daily for revival in our lives and in our church.

Signed: _____ "

Use of Prayer Lists

1. Ten Most Wanted List

The pastor prepares a list of ten people he really wants to help become Christians. Several weeks before the revival, he should send a copy to the evangelist who joins him in prayer. Hopefully, these are people the two of them will visit during the revival week in an effort to win them.

The pastor should ask deacons and other church members to make their own prayer lists and share copies with him. He joins them in prayer for the people on their lists.

2. Sunday School Prayer Lists

Teachers and department directors of grades four through adult are encouraged to search their class and department records for unsaved, unchurched and uninvolved members. They should also check the prospect file for other names in their age group. This should be done six weeks to two months before the revival meeting.

Workers with preschoolers through the third grade should search their records for parents who are unsaved, unchurched or inactive. These should be on their prayer lists.

Encourage teachers to visit, witness to, and invite these people to come with them to the revival services one or more evenings.

Prayer Retreats

This could be scheduled for Friday and Saturday three to four weeks before the revival meeting. It might be for deacons, church staff, and spouses. Sunday School departments, mission organizations, and other groups might plan a prayer retreat. Young people especially respond to this.

Enlist a committee to plan and promote the retreat. The program should include Bible study, prayer time by small groups, testimonies, recreation, and entertainment. Make it inspirational and entertaining.

7

Ideas on How to Reach the Unsaved, Unchurched, and Uninvolved Church Members

Three things are needed to do this: locate them, visit them, and telephone them.

Locate Unsaved and Unchurched Prospects

The single biggest problem in pre-revival visitation planning is that many churches don't have enough good prospects in the file to utilize the visitation teams that can be enlisted. Another problem is that the prospect file is worn out or outdated. Before the unsaved and unchurched can be reached, we must know their names and addresses.

Consider this formula. You need about sixty prospective families in your file for every one hundred people you average in attendance in Sunday School. If you don't have that many, you must locate them. Here are some ways.

1. Update the Prospect File.

Eliminate the names of those who have moved or joined other churches. Add the names of recent visitors in church services, newcomers to the community, unsaved or unchurched parents of Vacation Bible School children, and so forth. Get the file ready for use.

2. Do a Roll Search.

Examine the Sunday School and church rolls and records. Locate the unsaved people on your Sunday School rolls. Locate unsaved and unchurched people in the families of church members and Sunday School members. These are some of your best prospects. Add these to the prospect file.

3. Take an Inside Survey.

Prepare "I Know a Prospect" cards. Include this information on them:
Name _____
Address _____
Phone _____
Approximate Age _____
Christian: Yes___ No___
Church Member: Yes___ No___
Family _____
Signed: _____

Set aside one or two Sundays about five to eight weeks before your revival meeting. During the Sunday School or worship service give adults and youth one or more "I Know a Prospect" cards. Ask them to share the names and information about unsaved and unchurched relatives, friends, neighbors, associates, classmates, and others. Add these names to the prospect file.

4. Conduct a Telephone Survey.

Secure family religious survey cards and a city directory. Check with the city hall or chamber of commerce about the directory. You need the names and phone numbers of people by streets and house numbers. Select the area you want to call. Enlist callers and assign them about thirty to fifty families to call. Eliminate commercial numbers.

The best times to call are Saturdays and Sundays or early in the evening of other days.

5. Do a Door-to-Door Census.

Use family religious survey cards. Enlist and assign canvassers to a square block or streets to survey. Saturday and Sunday are good for this.

6. Survey the Ten Nearest Houses.

Ask active church members to take a census at the ten houses nearest to theirs. This will not only produce some good prospects but it will also help members to become better acquainted with their neighbors and their spiritual condition. Provide family religious survey cards for this.

7. Subscribe to Newcomer Services.

In most cities and towns there is a newcomer service. They secure names from utility companies of new hookups. They visit the families and secure information. They make lists of new families with the information. Sometimes the lists also include denominational preference.

8. Secure a Good Resource Book on How to Conduct Religious Surveys.

Check your Christian book store or denominational headquarters for such a book.

Visitation

Consider two special weeks of visitation just before the revival meeting. Week two is given to visiting less active members. During week one concentrate on visiting prospective families. The first three of the following plans are variations of this.

1. Special Prerevival Visitation Teams

This is a plan I used very successfully in my pastorates. I also wrote it into some of my revival plan books. Hundreds of churches have used it and testify that it is simple and effective.

The pastor (or pastor and visitation chairperson or pastor and Sunday School director) prepares a list of everyone he thinks might visit for the revival. He writes them, explains the plans, and asks them to participate. Mail the letter about five to six weeks before the revival meeting.

Set a goal to enlist ten two-people teams for every one hundred in average Sunday School attendance. A team consists of two persons: husbands and wives or two men or two women.

During week four call all those to whom letters were mailed. In smaller churches, the pastor will do the calling. In larger churches, the pastor will enlist others to make the calls for him. The church secretary or visitation committee might do the calling. They should begin their conversation, "I'm calling in the pastor's behalf to find out if you and your wife (or husband) can serve as a visitation team." Usually more people will say yes to the pastor than anyone else. Secure their answer to participate. Pair up those who need a partner other than husband and wife.

During the week prepare assignment cards. You need four to six less active families to assign each team to visit two weeks before the revival meeting. You will also need four to six prospective families to assign each team during week one.

Two Sundays before the revival week conduct assignment session number one. Give brief instructions, then assign each team four to six less active church families to visit. Encourage them to visit their assigned families at least two times when it is most convenient to them.

One Sunday before the revival week follow similar procedure and assign prospective families to be visited during the week.

Provide child care one or two evenings and on Saturday.

As an alternative you might schedule two specific times for visitation each week. Consider one evening of the week and Saturday morning or Sunday afternoon. Make assignments each time.

Encourage visitation teams to invite

Ideas on How to Reach the Unsaved, Unchurched, and Uninvolved Church Members

those they visit to come with them to one of the revival services. Make it "bringatation."

2. Sunday School Prerevival Visitation

This is a variation of the above plan except you work it through the Sunday School. Enlist teachers to visit. Sign them up. Encourage them to sign up class members to join them. This needs to be done at least a month before the revival week.

Promote this visitation through the Sunday School and from the pulpit. Set a goal to have fifteen to twenty people visiting for every one hundred you average in Sunday School attendance.

It is best if teachers and class members visit those in their own age group.

3. Deacons Visit Less active members; Sunday School Visits Prospects

This is also a variation of plan 1. This is especially a good idea if you have a deacon family ministry program where each deacon is assigned fifteen or so families to whom he is to minister. Ask the deacons to be responsible for visiting less active members week two before the revival meeting. They may visit the less active families of those already assigned to them or be given assignments. They should visit at least twice during the week.

Ask the Sunday School director to lead teachers and class members to visit prospective families the week just before revival meeting. Schedule two times to visit, one evening and Saturday morning or Sunday afternoon.

4. Pastor, Church Staff, and Evangelistic Team Visitation

This is a must if you expect to see lost people saved during the revival meeting. In most of the revivals I planned through the years in my churches, the evangelist and I won many of those who made public professions of faith. On the other hand, I have preached in revival meetings in which the pastor and I made few or no soul-winning visits. Usually there were very few saved in those meetings. This is inexcusable.

Pastors and staff members need to constantly have numerous unsaved people they are cultivating to win. If you don't have fifteen or more lost men and women on your prayer list whom you are cultivating, you need to get with it now. Make revival meeting a time of harvesting. Have the evangelist visit these people with you.

Consider these suggestions for visiting with the evangelistic team during the revival week.

a. Plan carefully the times when you and the staff will visit with the team. Four o'clock to six-thirty in most areas is the best time for this, especially in large cities. Eat after the services. Don't use up the most valuable visitation time with meals. Visit unsaved children and youth after school, with permission of their parents. Visit adults after work hours. Try to visit at least one unsaved adult each evening. In smaller towns and rural areas visits can be made during the daytime.

b. Before you pick up one of the evangelists to go visiting, know exactly where you intend to visit. Locate the addresses on the map. Keep your visits in the same area to avoid using up your time traveling.

c. Always have more than enough people to visit because some are not going to be home.

d. Consider making appointments with people you plan to visit. This will save time and also assist you in visiting those most interested.

e. Spend some time in prayer with the evangelist before starting out to visit.

f. During the visits, introduce the evangelist and let him do the witnessing. Study his technique to see how you can improve your witnessing. When I was a young pastor, I learned more about witnessing from my evangelists than from any other source.

5. Operation Andrew

This is an idea used so very effectively by the Billy Graham Evangelistic Association. It is a plan to involve active, dedicated Christians in bringing unsaved and unchurched people to the revival services. It is based on John 1:40-42: "One of the two who heard John speak, and followed him [Jesus], was Andrew, Simon Peter's brother. He first found his brother Simon, and said to him, 'We have found the Messiah' (which means Christ). He brought him to Jesus."

The reason more people are not saved in most of our evangelistic campaigns is because we do not have enough unsaved people present. Since most people who make decisions for Christ are brought by someone, we must get our members working on this. Operation Andrew or something similar must be put into action early.

The five steps in Operation Andrew are:
(1) Begin to pray for one to ten unsaved persons.
(2) Cultivate their friendship.
(3) Bring them to the revival services.
(4) Encourage them to commit their lives to Christ.
(5) Follow up with them until they are actively involved with a church.

The pastor is primarily responsible for this plan, but he should definitely involve the Sunday School. Perhaps the Sunday School director should be cochairman.

Ideally, it would be good to have Operation Andrew functioning at least two months before the revival meeting. So you need to begin enlistment about three months before your revival week. On the next page you have an "Operation Andrew Calendar" with an "Operation Andrew Survey" form on the reverse side. Use these in your planning.

6. Prayertations

This is a combination cottage prayer meeting and visitation. Thirty minutes are spent in prayer, visitation assignments are made, and about forty-five minutes are spent visiting. This idea is developed in chapter 6, "Ideas on How to Prepare the Church Spiritually for Revival."

7. All-Church Luncheon and Visitation

On the Sunday the revival meeting begins, have a light meal ready to serve right after the morning worship service. Then make assignments quickly and spend a couple hours visiting. Encourage the people who visit to invite those being visited to come with them to the service that evening or one evening during the week. Provide child care for grade school and preschool children.

You might prefer to have a lunch or brunch on Saturday before the revival for this visitation.

Be sure to have plenty of prospects to visit. Nothing will defeat this visitation plan quicker than the lack of good prospects.

8. Assign Prospects by Correspondence

The pastor, or pastor and Sunday School director, should send a letter of explanation to people whom they know will visit. Include the names, addresses, and phone numbers of people to be visited the week or two before the revival meeting. Encourage the people doing the visiting to bring the people they visit with them to the revival services. Assign unsaved people to members who are soul-winners.

9. Pastor-Assigned Visitation

The pastor personally calls several members whom he knows to be soul-

Operation Andrew Calendar

	Sunday	Monday	Tuesday	Wednesday	Thursday	Friday	Saturday
12 WEEKS BEFORE REVIVAL WEEK	Make a list of all the people you would like to invite to participate in Operation Andrew. Send a letter to each one explaining operation Andrew and asking them to participate. You might want to include your Sunday school director in this and make it a Sunday School project. Either way, be sure to enlist Sunday school workers in Operation Andrew. Also include deacons and other church leaders.						
11 WEEKS BEFORE REVIVAL WEEK	Begin enlistment of Operation Andrew participants. Call all of those to whom a letter was sent and get their answer. In larger churches the pastor (and Sunday school director) should probably make the calls. In smaller churches the pastor's secretary of a committee can be enlisted to make the calls. They should begin their phone conversation like this: "I'm calling in behalf of the pastor to find out if you plan to participate in Operation Andrew." Usually more people will say yes to the pastor than anyone else.						
10 WEEKS BEFORE REVIVAL WEEK	Complete enlistment of participants in Operation Andrew. Be sure all the people to whom you sent letters are called personally. This works best in enlistment. Make copies of **"Operation Andrew Survey"** form. (See reverse side.)		Put an article in the church newsletter about Operation Andrew Briefing.		Have all participants in Operation Andrew called and reminded of the briefing on Sunday. Put an article in Sunday's bulletin about briefing.		
9 WEEKS BEFORE REVIVAL WEEK	Conduct Operation Andrew Briefing. Give each participant a copy of the "Operation Andrew Survey" form. Review it with them. Start with circle number two. Ask them to write down the names of all unsaved people in the immediate family. Do this for each circle, one at a time. After the survey is completed, ask them to begin praying for these people daily. Encourage them to visit periodically with these people. Take them out to lunch. Go by and have coffee with them. Play golf with them. Etc. Share ideas on how to cultivate and witness to unsaved people. Conduct progress meetings about every two or three weeks. On the Sunday the revival meeting begins, meet with Operations Andrew participants and the evangelist.						

OPERATION ANDREW

Survey*

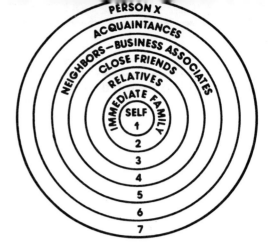

In the blank spaces below, write the names of people you know to be unsaved or unchurched and the names of people whom you do not know whether they are Christians or not.

Start with concentric circle #2, "Immediate Family". Think of everyone in the circle, then write the names unsaved, unchurched, or persons about whom you are unsure. Repeat the processes for circles #3, #4, etc.

_____   _____
_____   _____
_____   _____
_____   _____
_____   _____
_____   _____
_____   _____
_____   _____
_____   _____
_____   _____
_____   _____
_____   _____

God helping me, I will pray daily for each of the above, cultivate their friendship, bring them to the services, encourage them to commit their lives to Christ, and help to follow up their decision.

Date _____   Signed _____

Carry this in your Bible as a daily prayer reminder, or place it in a conspicuous place to remind you.

*The concentric circle above was taken from this book: W. Oscar Thompson, Jr., *Concentric Circles of Concern* (Nashville: Broadman Press, 1981), p. 21. This would be an excellent book to read in preparation for Operation Andrew.

winners. He asks them to join him in special prerevival visitation and witnessing. The pastor shares with them the names of one or more unsaved persons. They are to begin immediately praying for the people assigned to them. They are to visit them, witness to them, and bring them to the revival services. You need to begin this at least three to four weeks before the revival meeting.

10. Women's Visitation During Revival Week

Schedule visitation during the daytime for women who do not work outside the home. Ask them to meet at the church at ten o'clock in the morning to go visiting in teams of twos. Give each team three or four prospects to visit. They might call to make appointments.

11. Teacher-Led Visitation

Assignment cards are sent to each Sunday School class to be distributed on Sunday morning. The teacher will make assignments to class members who will visit those assigned to them during the week.

On two Sundays before the revival meeting, assign less active class members to be visited. The next Sunday assign prospects, especially those in the age group of the class.

12. Nightly Assigned Visitation During the Revival Week

Ask active members to remain for a few moments after the first evening revival service. Give each member an envelope with two prospects to be contacted before the next evening. The members might make their visits on the way home from the revival service. They might visit on their way to the services the next evening. Each evening thereafter, assignment cards of those visited will be returned with remarks and new assignments will be made.

Telephone Campaign

Do this before every revival meeting. It is a great way to get the word out the fastest and to the most people.

Select a committee to be responsible for enlisting a telephone crew. They will call all church families and prospective families, encouraging them to participate in the revival effort. In small communities, you might take the phone book and call every family in the area.

If you have less than 150 families to call, the chairperson enlists one caller for every 15 families to be called. If you have over 150 families to call, enlist one committee member for every 150 families to be called. They in turn will enlist 10 callers each. For example, if you have 450 families to be called, then the chairperson enlists three committee members. They enlist 10 callers each and that makes 30 callers. If they each make 15 calls, then 450 families will be called. It is good to have a committee member from each adult department who will enlist 10 callers from his or her department.

Enlist youth callers to call young people.

This plan is developed in detail in the telephone chairperson's instructions in the completed plan.

8

Ideas on How to Build Attendance

You need plans to build the attendance throughout the revival week. Here are some good ways to do that.

Sunday School Rally Night on Monday

I use some variety of this in almost every one of my revival plans to build a crowd for Monday evening. It is imperative that the first week night revival service be well attended. In some revival meetings the Monday night crowd could all be seated in the choir loft. That is a terrible way to begin. Since Monday is such a hard night to build attendance, use your biggest and best organization to build the attendance for this most important service.

Give the responsibility to a Sunday School committee with the Sunday School director as chairperson. Department directors or class teachers will serve on the committee.

Plan to have every teacher to sign up his or her class members to be present on Monday evening. Use a sign-up card with this information printed on it:

SUNDAY SCHOOL RALLY NIGHT
"Yes, I will attend the Monday evening revival service to help represent my department/class in a big way."
Signed _____

You might prefer to have a sign-up sheet for each class with the same information at the top and places to sign below.

Classes or departments might or might not sit together in designated areas of the auditorium. If they sit together, place a small banner on pews to mark the places where they are to sit. Early in the service recognize departments/classes and workers. Brag on them. You might have a contest to see which department/class has the best attendance or highest percentage present. Don't take too much time in the service with counting and recognition. If departments/classes sit together, have small children go and sit with parents after the recognition.

In one of my plans, I call this "Church Loyalty Night." In another plan book, I promote it as "Battle of the Banners." Each department/class sits together near its banner. Recognize those with highest attendance and percentage.

This plan is developed in detail in the Sunday School chairperson's instructions in the completed plan of Section III.

Youth Emphasis One Night

Schedule an event for youth one hour before the revival service early in the week. Don't call this "Youth Night" because some adults will think the service is just for youth.

Enlist a youth committee chairperson from workers with youth in Sunday School. The minister of youth might be chairperson. Other workers with youth in Sunday School will serve on the committee.

The event might be a pizza supper. It could be a spaghetti dinner or a taco feast. In one revival meeting in which I preached, the youth event featured "The World's Longest Submarine Sandwich." They used long loaves of French bread placed end to end with meat and cheese inside. The sandwich was cut in small individual pieces. One church served a "Fifty-Five-Foot Banana Split." In the

Ideas on How to Build Attendance

completed plan, I call this event a "Youth Joy Explosion," which can be almost anything you want it to be.

Consider inviting a guest personality like a well-known athlete, beauty contestant, or musical group. Be sure that it is someone that unsaved and unchurched youth would like to see and hear.

Only one hour is needed for the event. Use about twenty minutes for serving and eating. Take about twenty minutes for some good entertainment. Give the evangelist about ten minutes to talk with the youth about how to become Christians. This is no time for a sermon. Hopefully some of these young people will make professions of faith in the revival service. This is the reason the youth event should be scheduled before the service rather than afterwards.

If you use a guest personality, give them about twenty minutes after the meal to share. He or she should begin with something entertaining and conclude with a personal Christian testimony. Use the guest personality to share briefly in the revival service.

Have young people sit together in the service and recognize them as special guests.

To build the attendance, send a letter and five tickets to each young person who is either a member or a prospect. Encourage the young people to give the tickets to friends and bring them to the event. Printing on the ticket should include church, location, date, time, and any special feature. Be sure to print the time the event begins and the revival service ends, like 6:30-8:45. If you don't, youth might go home after the event and not stay for the revival service.

Promote this event in youth departments and in church newsletters. Ask youth to make posters.

This plan is presented in detail in the youth chairperson's instructions in the completed plan of Section III.

Children's Event One Night

Schedule this one hour before the revival service. Don't call it "Children's Night" because other age groups might think the revival service is for children only.

Enlist a children's committee chairperson from workers with children in Sunday School. Other workers with children will serve on the committee.

The event might be a hot dog or corn dog supper. You could call it "Children's Hour" and do a variety of things.

Use about twenty minutes for serving and eating. Allow fifteen minutes for fun time. Consider a special feature like a puppet show or a magic show. You might use a ventriloquist or a clown. Leave about ten minutes for the evangelist to talk briefly to the boys and girls about Jesus. This is no time for a sermon or invitation. Hopefully some of the children will make professions of faith in the service that is to follow, but avoid pressure.

Have children sit together in the revival service and recognize them as special guests.

To build attendance, send a letter and five tickets to each boy and girl who is either a member of Sunday School or is a prospect. Encourage children to give the tickets to friends and classmates and bring them to the event. Printing on the tickets should include church, location, date, time, and special feature. Be sure to print the time the event begins and the revival service ends, like 6:30-8:45. This will keep children from going home after the event. It will also inform parents exactly how long the children will be at the church.

Promote this event in the children's Sunday School departments. Have children make posters to advertise the event. You might have a poster contest.

This plan is developed in detail in the

children's chairperson's instructions in the completed plan of Section III.

Men and Women's Night

Have one night especially for men and women. You might have an all-church dinner before the service or an all-church fellowship after the service. If you have the dinner, ask adults to bring friends with them and make it a prospect dinner. The fellowship might be a homemade ice-cream supper. Do something especially entertaining for adults.

Enlist a worker with adults in Sunday School to be chairperson of the "Adult Committee." Use other workers with adults on the committee. Promote this in adult departments in Sunday School. You might send a card or letter of invitation to all adults, members, and prospects.

This plan is developed in detail in the adult chairperson's instructions in the completed plan of Section III.

Young Adult Soup and Sandwich Supper

If you have a good number of this age group, plan a meal for them one hour before the service one evening.

Enlist someone who works with this age group in Sunday School to be chairperson of the committee. Other workers with young adults and some of the young adults should also serve on the committee. They are responsible for planning the meal and promoting attendance.

Keep the meal simple, such as soup and sandwiches, soup and salad, spaghetti, corn bread and beans, or chili.

Send a letter to all young adults who are members or prospects. Strongly encourage them to bring guests with them. Promote this in the Sunday School departments of young adults. Assign prospective young adults to members and ask them to bring them to the supper.

After the meal, have a few minutes of good entertainment. You may want to ask some of the young adults to share Christian testimonies. Give the evangelist ten to twelve minutes to share with them.

Have the young adults sit together in the revival service and recognize them as special guests that evening.

Single Adult Spaghetti Supper

Organize it as suggested above for young adults. You might have a meal one place for young singles, like college and career, and another place for older singles.

Senior Adult Old-Fashioned Pie Supper

This is a good idea for Friday evening, especially in the fall months when football games conflict with services.

Schedule the Old-Fashioned Pie Supper one hour before the revival service. The committee could ask an appropriate number of people to bring pies. The church should provide tea and coffee.

Select a chairperson and committee from workers with senior adults in Sunday School. They are responsible for promoting attendance. One week before the event they should send a letter to all senior adults inviting them to attend and bring guests. Two days before the event they should call all senior adults encouraging them to attend. They should also offer to provide transportation for those who need it.

The program should include a word from the evangelist. Consider special music by senior adults. Ask some of them to share their Christian testimonies.

Have them sit together in the revival service and give them special recognition. The music that night should include some old-time favorites. You might combine it with "Old-Fashioned Night."

Family Night

Friday is a good evening for this. You might ask the deacons to be responsible for this if you have a deacon family ministry program. The deacons and their

Ideas on How to Build Attendance

spouses should call the membership on Wednesday and Thursday urging attendance at Family night.

In some of my plans, I assign this responsibility to the telephone committee and call it a contact committee. That is what I did in the completed plan of Section III. The committee should mail invitation cards to arrive in the homes on Wednesday and Thursday.

Encourage members to invite relatives to come and sit together. Many times unsaved fathers or husbands will accompany families to this event. So will other unsaved relatives. You might recognize the family with the largest number of relatives present. The pastor should promote this in all the evening services.

You might have something like an old-fashioned ice-cream fellowship after the service.

Music Night

This is a good event for Saturday evening if you have services that night. Friday is also a good night for this.

Use as many of your choirs, ensembles, quartets, and soloists as possible. Be sure to use the children's choirs because parents will come to hear their own.

If the music evangelist is a good soloist, he might present a miniconcert prior to the sermon. Guest musical groups might be invited.

The music committee should also assume this responsibility.

Old-Fashioned Night

Encourage members to dress in old-fashioned clothes. Use lanterns or lamps to light the building. Sing old favorite hymns. Plan an old-fashioned pie supper or homemade ice-cream feed after the service.

Good Neighbor Night

Ask the visitation committee to assume this responsibility too. All revival visitation teams should bring guests with them to the service. Encourage members to bring friends, neighbors, relatives, classmates, and fellow workers. Assign unsaved and unchurched people to members who try to bring these people with them to the revival service. Promote this earlier in the revival week.

High Attendance Day in Sunday School

You can plan this for the first or last Sunday, but the last Sunday is probably the best. The pastor promotes this each evening in the revival services. It gives him an opportunity to talk about the importance of Sunday School. "Revival Attendance Envelopes" can be ordered from your favorite book store for this. Included on the envelope are these words: "Count on me for high attendance in Sunday School." Those in attendance are asked to check the blank beside the statement.

You may choose to schedule high attendance on the first Sunday to get the revival meeting off to a good start. Start on this two weeks earlier.

You need some kind of sign-up plan to get the best attendance possible. You might use commitment cards with wording something like this printed on them:

SUNDAY SCHOOL HIGH
ATTENDANCE DAY
"Yes, I will do my best to be in Sunday School next Sunday."
Signed _____

Teachers are responsible to sign up all class members and prospects. Ask members to sign up during Sunday School, then absentees will be called and asked for permission to sign them up.

You might choose to use a "Sunday School Petition." At the top of the pages print something like this: SUNDAY SCHOOL PETITION: "Yes, I will do my best to attend Sunday School next Sunday." Members are asked to sign it and secure the signatures of absentees and prospects.

Several years ago we used chain links to sign up people for high attendance in Sunday School. Small 1- by 8½-inch strips of paper contained words like this: "I will do my best to attend Sunday School next Sunday." Signed _____

After being signed, these are to be stapled or taped together as links of a chain. Each department or class has its own chain. These are displayed in a prominent place, such as the auditorium, under a sign with the department or class name printed on it. It only takes a quick glance to see if a department or class is working at this. Short chains ought to cause the people in that age group to get busy. Teachers and class members are responsible for signing up their members and prospects.

Children's Jamboree

Schedule thirty minutes before each evening service to meet with children. Enlist a children's committee and chairperson from Sunday School workers with children. Each evening serve light refreshments. Have a contest. Award points for attendance, guests they bring, memory verses recited, bringing parents to services, and so forth. At the end of the week, reward the winners with something special.

You might call this "Pastor's Pals" with the pastor in charge each evening. He will also promote this himself in the children's departments and classes.

One evangelist called it "Country Store." Children earned points as mentioned above. With these they were able to purchase small gifts at the country store.

Select memory verses that are easy to memorize and that teach boys and girls about Jesus, how to be saved, and how to treat others.

Pack-a-Pew Plan

A few years ago this was a most successful way to build attendance for revival meetings. It will still work effectively if it is properly organized and the people are motivated to work hard at it.

Schedule Monday night to be Sunday School Rally Night. Then the youth are given Tuesday night to pack-a-pew. Adults are assigned Wednesday and children are given Thursday. The Sunday School committee is responsible for Monday, then the youth, adult, and children's committees are responsible for the nights designated for their age groups.

Each committee will enlist pew captains from their departments or classes. Use both Sunday School teachers and pupils. Pew captains will be asked to sign commitment cards. The printed card should include these words: "Because I want to help build the revival attendance, I will serve as a pew captain and do my best to pack my pew on the night assigned to me. Signed _____."

Be sure each pew captain knows which pew is his or hers. You might draw a big diagram of the auditorium and write the pew captains' names on it. Each evening be sure that a small card with the pew captain's name on it is taped to the pew assigned to him or her.

Recognize pew captains each evening and brag on them. Don't embarrass those who have only a few people.

Assign to pew captains the names of one or two prospects for them to enlist to sit on their pew.

You might choose to assign nights like this: men, women, youth, and children.

Another variation is to use the pack-a-pew plan for one night only. Enlist a committee to enlist pew captains.

Host with the Most

Hosts and hostesses are enlisted to be responsible for bringing ten or more peo-

Ideas on How to Build Attendance

ple with them to the revival services on assigned nights. Be sure you have enough hosts and hostesses to build a crowd equal to your average Sunday School or Sunday morning attendance.

Enlist adult, youth, and children's committees composed of Sunday School workers with each age group. Assign one night each to adults, youth, and children. You might assign the adults two nights, one for men and one for women.

During the service, recognize the hosts and hostesses, especially the one who brought the most. You might award winners a blue ribbon. Make it fun and challenging.

Assign hosts and hostesses the names of two prospects each to invite to attend with them on their assigned nights.

Use Guest Personalities

Secure well-know personalities, such as athletes, beauty contestants, and musical performers. They should be asked to share their Christian testimonies. Allot them about ten minutes, no more than fifteen minutes; otherwise the service will be too lengthy.

Be sure to secure personalities whom unsaved and unchurched people would like to see and hear. Publicize their appearance. Get them on television talk shows if possible, in school assemblies, or service clubs.

Victory Celebration Fellowship

Plan a big all-church fellowship after the last revival service of the week. Enlist families to bring freezers of homemade ice cream or cakes. Express appreciation to the evangelistic team, as well as revival chairpersons and committee members. Promote this throughout the week. Make it a big and exciting event.

Prospect Dinner or All-Church Dinner

If your church already serves a meal on Wednesday, this is a natural for that time. You might plan a potluck dinner.

Members are to bring unsaved, unchurched, and uninvolved church members with them to the dinner as special guests. You might assign to members the names of prospects to bring with them.

C.I.F. Fellowship for Youth

C.I.F. stands for "Christianity Is Fun." Schedule this for Friday evening after the service. Make it a good, fun event and publicize it. You want to attract lots of youth for the revival service that evening.

Do not let this take the place of a youth event on Tuesday. Do both. If you do only one, then go with the youth event on Tuesday. It is important to get youth in the services early in the week.

Meet the Revival Team Fellowship

Schedule this for the first Sunday evening after the revival service. You might prefer to have a church meal on Saturday with the evangelistic team present. Encourage Sunday School teachers to promote this during Sunday School. Announce it in the Sunday bulletin and at the announcement time.

9

Ideas on How to Publicize Revival Meetings

All publicity ideas play a supportive role to personal contacts. The very best publicity is personal, people telling people about the revival meeting. This should include assigned visitation or phone calls, casual and intentional contacts. Few people outside the church will attend a revival meeting just because they saw or heard some of the publicity. It will make them aware of the meeting, but it will still take personal contacts to get most unsaved, unchurched, and uninvolved members present.

Following are a variety of ideas to assist you in getting the word out about your revival meeting.

Use of Theme in Publicity

Have a common theme for revival publicity. If the poster, visitation leaflets, and yard signs, all have the same theme and logo, even the quickest glance will eventually remind people about the revival meeting. For examples, look at the artwork provided in the latter part of this chapter and the publicity chairperson's instructions in the completed plan of Section III.

Posters

Keep the information on the posters brief. You want people to be able to read it as they walk by. On posters to be put up on the church building, print only the revival dates and times of services. If the names of the evangelists are well known, include these. On posters to be used in the community, be sure to add the church name and location.

You might be able to secure revival posters at religious book stores or from the evangelism department of your denominational offices. You overprint your revival information on most of these prepared posters.

You can have your own posters printed. A good size is 11 by 14 inches or 11 by 17 inches. These can be reproduced on most offset presses. At the end of this chapter and in the publicity chairperson's instructions in the completed plan, I have provided artwork which can be enlarged and reproduced.

You might enlist some artistic people to prepare attractive posters. They can use poster boards and felt tip markers. Have a poster contest among the children. Display all their posters. They always attract attention, especially if the people know the children.

Put up posters in the church buildings about three weekends before the revival meeting. Put up posters in community store windows and on school bulletin boards about ten days before the revival week. Be sure to ask for permission to put the posters up, then take them down after the last revival service.

Visitation Leaflets

Revival visitation teams need leaflets which contain the church name, location, revival dates, and time of services to give to the people they visit. If no one is at home, they need to leave the leaflet with a personal note. Members also need leaflets to give as invitations to their neighbors, friends, associates, and classmates.

The size should be 5½ × 8½ inches, which is half of a letter size page. On one side print the revival theme and logo. On

Ideas on How to Publicize Revival Meetings

the reverse side print the revival information. At the end of this chapter artwork is provided for leaflets. Also in the publicity chairperson's instructions in the completed plan other artwork is provided for leaflets.

These leaflets can also be used as circulars to pass out door to door in the community. They can be used as inserts in the Sunday bulletins.

Promotion in Church Newsletters

If the church mails a newsletter to members, the letter should be used to advertise the revival events.

Start publicizing the revival dates about a month or more before the week of services. Give the names of revival chairpersons. Then promote preparation events, such as revival visitation, and prayer meetings. Be sure the schedule for the revival week is included in the issue just before the meeting begins.

Use pictures of evangelists if you can. Give a brief biographical sketch of them.

Announcements in Sunday Bulletins

Be sure revival events are printed in the announcement section of your bulletins. Print the revival schedule on the Sunday the revival meeting begins.

Correspondence

1. Letter from Pastor to Prospects

Make the letter as personal as time and money will permit. A typed letter, signed by the pastor, and mailed with first-class postage will get the best reading. You might offset print the body of the letter and type in the name and address. Less effective, but still good, is a printed letter sent by bulk mail.

You might put "Don't forward; return to sender" on the envelope. It will cost you extra, but it will help you to clean up your prospect file.

Mail the letters the week just before the revival meeting. It is best if prospects receive the letters on Friday or Saturday.

2. Letter from Evangelist to Church Members

Have the evangelist write a letter to the church members on his stationery. Ask the secretary to reproduce the letter. If you can secure or purchase the envelopes to his stationery, it will attract more attention than your church's. First-class postage is best, but if you need to, use the bulk permit.

Mail the letters the week before the revival meeting. They need to arrive on Friday or Saturday.

3. Letter-Writing Campaign

Assign members names of persons to write, especially unsaved or unchurched persons and inactive members. Ask them to write to friends and relatives, inviting them to the revival services.

4. Mail Out to Community

You might send a letter or card to every mailing address in your community. Be sure it is brief and well written.

Newspapers

1. News Releases

Prepare news articles about the revival meeting. Include pictures of evangelists. Most newspapers will print these for you. If you are using well-known guest personalities, be sure to give the papers this information and pictures.

Take news releases to the newspapers on Monday or Tuesday of the week before the revival meeting. You might call to be sure about deadlines. Ask them to print the news releases on Friday or Saturday.

2. Paid Advertisement

You will probably get more free publicity if you also buy some advertisement. One or two column ads, 4 to 8 inches in length, will probably be adequate. Use pictures. Give the church name, location, revival dates, and times of services. Don't overcrowd the ads. At the end of this chapter and in the publicity chairperson's instruction in the completed plan, artwork is provided for paid newspaper advertisement.

The best times for these ads are the last of the week before the revival meeting and the first few days of the revival week.

Radio and Television

1. Free Advertisement

Many stations have community announcement times, especially in smaller cities and towns. Provide the stations with a simple and brief written announcement.

Some television cables have a station that provides printed announcements. Some have a rotating camera that shows time, temperature, etc. Sometimes you can put one of your posters in the rotation.

2. Paid Advertisement

Check with stations about this. Get someone who is knowledgeable in radio and television advertisement to assist you.

Run radio and television spots two or three days before the revival meeting starts and two or three days into the revival week.

3. Personality Interviews

Some television stations have daytime talk shows on which they interview people involved in special things. In a city where I pastored, we were always able to get our evangelistic team on the show. The music evangelist would usually sing a solo. I introduced the preacher who was given a chance to say a few things about our meeting. Sometimes he was given an opportunity to share a unique experience.

When we brought in big-name athletes, I was usually able to get the sports broadcaster to interview them and air it on the six o'clock news. Most of the people in our community watched the newscast so everybody heard about our meeting.

Churchyard Sign

Ask a carpenter to build a sign about 3 feet by 5 feet to be put up in the churchyard. Ask someone artistic to paint the sign and print the lettering. Keep the wording simple and brief. Make the letters big. The sign needs to be read as people drive by. Make it a two-way sign with wording on both sides.

You might hire a sign company to make a sign for you. Or you can rent a portable sign and put your own information on it.

If you have a sign at a main street to give directions to your church, put a sign there too.

These should be up about ten days before the revival meeting and be taken down right after the week is over.

Signs in Church Members' Yards

Make small signs like politicians put up in yards at election time. You can have these printed but it gets rather expensive. You can make your own by cutting a poster board in half and stapling them together with a stake in between. Make a stencil by cutting out the letters, then spray paint the wording on the signs.

These should be put up about seven to ten days before the revival week.

Door-to-Door Circulars

This is a good way to advertise a revival meeting and to advertise your church at the same time. Even if all of the people who receive the circulars don't come to the revival services, they have been made aware of your church. Later they may attend or send their children to your Vacation Bible School.

Ideas on How to Publicize Revival Meetings

You can use the visitation leaflets as described above for this. You might prefer to make a special circular.

Ask children's or youth workers to organize a crew to pass these out on Saturday before the revival week.

Billboards

There are various sizes of outdoor billboards. Usually sign companies rent these by the month. It gets pretty expensive, but check it out.

You might rent portable signs and place them near heavy traffic patterns.

You might construct your own junior billboards, using 4- by 8-feet plywood.

Keep the wording on billboards simple and brief so that it can be read at a glance.

Street Banners

In smaller cities and towns, you might be able to secure permission to put up a banner across a main street. Probably you ought to secure a sign company to make the banner for you. Keep the wording simple and brief so it can be read quickly. Put these up about seven to eight days before the revival week and take them down after the last service.

Lapel or Book Stickers

You can secure sheets of colorful gummed labels from an office supplier. The revival information can be mimeographed or printed on the labels. You can even get a rubber stamp made with the revival information on it and print the stickers that way.

Cut the labels apart and give them out. People can peel the backing off and attach these to their clothing or to schoolbook covers.

Keep the wording very brief. In fact it would probably be best if you printed only a word or a symbol to cause people to ask what it means. For example the wording might be: "Hear Joe" or "Apr. 3-8" or "Ask Me" or something like that. When asked the meaning, members can tell about the revival meeting.

Begin using these about seven to eight days before the revival week. Youth and children especially like clever stickers.

Display the Revival Theme in the Church Auditorium

Cut letters and logo out of poster boards and attach them to a wall of the auditorium. You can cut letters out of Styrofoam, color or decorate them, and hang them on very fine wire stretched across the choir loft. Use your imagination to be creative. It needs to be up about ten days before your revival week.

You might prefer to make a display elsewhere in the church building.

Miscellaneous Ideas

1. Bulletin covers or inserts
2. Hymnbook covers
3. Bumper stickers
4. Poster in rear window of cars
5. Bible, New Testament or Scripture portion distribution with revival information
6. Ask store managers with marquees to advertise the revival dates.
7. Ask grocery store managers to put circulars in grocery bags or let you stamp your revival information on grocery bags.
8. Be creative. There are lots more ways to get the word out.

Note About Art Work on Following Pages

The "Victory in Jesus" material is the theme of one of the revival plans I wrote. The theme of the second one is "Church Crusade." Both were developed by Linda Kokel, an artist in the public relations department of the Baptist General Convention of Texas. They are used here by permission. You may reproduce these for personal use but not for resell.

In the completed plan of Section III another set of artwork is provided for you to use in your next revival meeting.

Victory in Jesus Revival

_____
(Church)

_____
(dates)

_____
(time)

Preacher

[picture]

_____
(name)

Singer

[picture]

_____
(name)

Victory in Jesus Revival

_____
(Church)

_____
(dates)

_____
(time)

Preacher

[picture]

_____
(name)

Singer

[picture]

_____
(name)

For Publicity Chairman

Ads for Newspaper and Church Newsletter

Simply deliver the ads to the newspaper accompanied with church information. They will add the print. For church newsletters that use offset, simply add the information yourself.

Church Crusade

_____
(Church)

_____
(dates)

_____
(time)

Preacher

[picture]

_____
(name)

Singer

[picture]

_____
(name)

Church Crusade

_____
(Church)

_____
(dates)

_____
(time)

Preacher

[picture]

_____
(name)

Singer

[picture]

_____
(name)

You are invited to the Church Crusade at the

You are invited to the Church Crusade at the

Ads for Newspaper and Church Newsletter

Simply deliver the ads to the newspaper accompanied with church information. They will add the print. For church newsletters that use offset, simply add the information yourself.

10

Ideas on How to Prepare for Counseling

It is imperative to use trained counselors. This is especially true if you expect very many people to come forward during the invitation at the conclusion of the sermon. When the pastor tries to handle it by himself, lines often form waiting to talk to him. And when the line starts forming, the people usually stop coming.

I remember one time that ten people came all at once on the first stanza of the invitation hymn. The pastor said that he wanted to be thorough, so he took three minutes with each one. That took thirty minutes. He was not thorough, and the invitation dragged on for thirty minutes. No one else came. He should have had laypersons ready to assist those who came forward.

I recall another time when several people were waiting to talk to the pastor, the person on the end of the line turned to go back to his seat. I did something that I don't do as an evangelist. I stepped off the platform just in time to catch the person and counsel with him. He accepted Christ as his Savior.

Pastors need to use laypersons to help counsel those who make public decisions during invitations.

Enlisting Counselors

Choose your best laypersons. They must be people who are respected by others, morally pure, and are committed to God. If you have experienced soul-winners, use them. Members who have had lay witness training make good counselors.

You need two to three men and two to three women for every one hundred people you average in Sunday School attendance.

Materials for Counseling

You may already have materials or would prefer to develop your own. Your denominational evangelism office may have materials which can be ordered. A number of very good witnessing booklets are available. Check with your Christian book store and decide on the one best suited for your people.

Counselors simply read through the booklets with those wanting to receive Jesus as Savior. The counselor leads the inquirer to pray either the prayer in the booklet or his own prayer to receive Jesus.

There are a number of counseling guides which can be ordered. Your Christian book store will be glad to help you find the right one for your use.

Mechanics of Counseling

The pastor normally should be the first one to receive those who come forward. If several come at once, other staff members might assist. Then after a few brief moments, the inquirer should be turned over to a trained counselor.

During revival meetings have one man counselor and one woman counselor come forward at the start of the invitation, ready to serve. As soon as one counselor is helping someone, another man or woman takes their place automatically. You might prefer for counselors to wait and come when you signal for them. This counseling can take place on the front pew or pews. People making decisions are usually presented to the church at the close of the service, except for children whose parents are not present.

If persons come to transfer membership, have a counselor to assist them. Before they fill out the decision card, the counselor should inquire about their salvation experience. If anyone has any doubts about his or her salvation, then the counselor should share the witnessing booklet with him or her.

You might prefer to use a counseling room where inquirers are taken for counseling. They could be returned to the service to be presented to the congregation or be presented later.

Training Counselors

It is imperative that you spend some time training counselors. They should know what you want them to do. They should know how to use the counseling materials. Periodically have review training sessions to deal with problems or questions. You might need to experiment until you find the plan and materials that best suit you.

Follow-up Counseling

Ask each counselor to follow up on the inquirers they assisted in the services. If you use a duplicate or triplicate decision card, give counselors one carbon copy. You might ask counselors to make notes for themselves with inquirer's name, address, and telephone number.

Counselors should check to be sure inquirers made the decisions they sought to make. Work with them until they know they are saved. Encourage them to follow through with baptism and to become active in Sunday School and worship services. Assist them as needed.

Counselors should provide watch care for new converts and new members for several weeks.

In the next chapter ways to do follow-up with new members will be presented.

11

Ideas on How to Do Follow-up with New Members

It is extremely important that all new members become active, growing, and serving Christians. This will not happen automatically with most people, so let's develop plans to assist them.

Immediate Follow-Up with New Converts

Within the week a person makes a public profession of faith, he or she should be visited by the pastor, a staff member, or a follow-up counselor. Make an appointment to visit in the person's home or to meet at the church. Parents of children should be present at such a visit.

Persons making visits should review the plan of salvation with the new members to make sure they have been saved. Don't take this for granted. Before you baptize them, be sure they have experienced genuine salvation. The meaning of baptism should be discussed. Plans should be made for their baptism. Set the date soon.

Immediate Contact by Sunday School Teachers

The very best follow-up plan for a new convert is a Bible-teaching, warmhearted Sunday School class.

Every new member should be contacted before the next Sunday by the Sunday School teacher of that age group. In some churches, the Sunday School teachers of new members are asked to come and stand with them when they are presented to the church. At that time, teachers should talk to the new members about attending class the next Sunday.

You need a system to communicate information about new members to Sunday School teachers. Work out the mechanics to see that this gets done within the week. A letter or phone call could do it. We need to get new members into Sunday School the very first Sunday after they join. The longer we delay, the less likely they are to attend Sunday School.

Be aware that new members who join the church but don't attend Sunday School are the most likely to drop by the wayside the quickest. Those who join and attend Sunday School are usually the ones who remain faithful the longest. So we owe it to our new members to get them into a good Sunday School class immediately.

Don't have a new member orientation class meeting during the Sunday School hour. New members need to be in their regular classes with their own age groups immediately after joining the church.

Special Follow-Up with Children and Youth

Extreme care should be taken with children. Before they are baptized, always review the plan of salvation with them to be sure they are saved. Ask questions which require more than yes or no answers.

Here is a good plan to use that will result in many unsaved parents coming to know Jesus as their Savior. After a child or young person makes a public profession of faith, make an appointment to meet with him or her and the parents. The mother and father need to know what you are doing with their child. Another reason for this is to give you an opportunity to witness to the parents. Many unsaved men will listen intently as you share the plan of salvation with their child when they would never let you talk to them directly about Christ.

For example, after a young lady made

her profession of faith, I called for an appointment. I asked for both parents to be present when I talked to their daughter. I knew the father was not a Christian and had not been very receptive to witnessing. When I visited in the home, I sat next to the daughter on the couch and explained salvation with the Bible. When I had completed my presentation and had prayer with the young lady, I turned my attention to the parents. First, I asked the mother if she had ever had an experience like this. When she answered in the affirmative, I asked her to tell me about it. She gave a beautiful testimony. Then I turned to the father who had been listening to it all and asked him, "Has this ever happened in your life?"

He shook his head and said, "No."

Then I asked, "You would like for this to happen in your life too wouldn't you?"

He paused and then said, "Yes." I went on to lead the man to Jesus. He made a public profession of faith and was baptized with his daughter.

I highly recommend this plan to you.

New Member's Packets

Provide a folder or package of materials to give to every new member or new family. Here is a list of things you might include in it:
1. Outline of church programs and schedule of events
2. A good tract on the plan of salvation
3. Tracts or brochures on baptism, doctrine, and so forth
4. Church directory
5. Church calendar
6. Church bylaws
7. Bible study or devotional guide
8. Offering envelopes

New Member Orientation Classes

Dr. L. L. Morris, who was a most successful pastor for many years and then became a state evangelism director, had an excellent plan. He and his minister of education conducted four orientation sessions each month. Session one was on the first Sunday of each month. Sessions two, three, and four were on the second, third, and fourth Sundays of each month. There was no class on the fifth Sunday. When people joined the church, they were enrolled in the new member orientation class immediately. It met prior to the Sunday evening worship service during the Church Training hour.

New members began with whatever session was being conducted and attended four Sunday evenings. If they were absent, this was to be made up the next month on that Sunday. The following Wednesday evening after they had completed the new member orientation, they were awarded a beautiful certificate during the midweek service. They were also given a chance to tell what the new member orientation had meant to them.

The subjects for the four sessions were:
1. The Christian experience (plan of salvation)
2. Distinctive doctrines
3. The mission and organizations of the church
4. The denomination

Most denominations provide good materials for new member orientation. These can be ordered along with Sunday School and Church Training literature.

Encourage Daily Bible Study and Prayer

This is private worship, and the primary means of worshiping God. Though public worship is very important, it has a supportive roll to private worship.

The two most important things Christians do are to read their Bibles and to pray daily. God talks to us through his Word. We talk to God in prayer. This is two-way communication and a most valuable part of Christian maturity.

So let's provide helps for this. There are some excellent material for new converts. Your Christian book store or denominational headquarters will be happy to help you.

Ideas on How to Do Follow-up with New Members

Watch Care Programs

This means assigning a mature, active Christian to work with new converts for a period of time. This is discipleship, and there are many good programs available for this. Do some research and plan a watch care program for your church.

Deacon Family Ministry Plan

Many churches are using this plan most successfully. When persons join the church, they are assigned to a deacon. That deacon is to minister to the family. He should visit them immediately and encourage them to become involved in the total life of the church. He should deliver the new member's packet and explain its contents. He should help them become acquainted with their new church and its programs.

After the initial visit, the deacon needs to provide watch care so that the new members don't drop by the wayside.

New Member Fellowships

Schedule periodic all-church fellowships or dinners to honor new members. Enlist all new members to be present. Don't just announce it and expect them to be there. Have a special recognition for them and make the event something exciting for all the church.

Section III
Completed Plan of Preparation for Your Next Revival Meeting

How To Use This Plan

Herein is contained a complete set of instructions to help you prepare for your next revival meeting. This plan is an example of planning as outlined in the first section and uses some of the ideas suggested in the second section.

Start planning at least ten to twelve weeks before your revival meeting.

Please don't let the size of the materials defeat you. The instructions for the General Chairman/Pastor are contained on two pages. With these pages you will know how to use all the rest of the materials. After your instructions, the following pages contain two copies of each chairman's instructions and art work to reproduce materials. You will give each chairman one copy and retain a copy in the book for your reference.

1. Read the "Brief Revival Overview" on the next page to acquaint yourself with the overall picture of the plans.

2. Look over the "Revival Steering Committee' on the following pages to see how you will organize your planning committee. Smaller churches may want to use fewer committees as suggested, but remember, the more people you involve, the better will be the end results.

3. Instructions for General Chairman/Pastor on the next pages tells how to enlist and train committee chairmen.

4. The rest of the General Chairman/Pastor's instructions are contained on his countdown calendar. Fill in the dates starting with your revival week and back up six weeks filling in the dates. Then you will have a tailor-made countdown calendar to guide you as you lead your church in revival preparation. You may want to make a copy of the calendar to keep on your desk top to guide you through the last six weeks of planning to keep you on schedule. <u>This is extremely important</u>.

5. Following the General Chairman/Pastor's instructions and calendar you have a Steering Committee Checklist. Everything that each chairman is supposed to do is listed. It will greatly help you to make sure the chairmen are getting their work done on schedule.

6. After the Steering Committee Checklist you have two copies of each chairman's instructions. They are in alphabetical order. One copy you will give to chairmen when you train them and keep the other copy for your reference. Also give each chairman the pages of art work to reproduce his materials. Briefly review their instructions and become familiar with them. Then train your chairmen as outlined in General Chairman/Pastor's instructions. <u>This training is extremely important</u>.

The best way to use the materials is to follow the plans as outlined, making only necessary changes. Please be aware of shortcuts that might result in a less effective effort.

BRIEF REVIVAL OVERVIEW

1. About seven weeks before the revival week the pastor trains the committee chairmen.

2. The Prayer Committee will lead the church to prepare spiritually for revival.

3. Visitation teams will be enlisted to visit less active members and prospects the two weeks prior to the revival week.

4. A telephone crew will call all the members and prospects the week before the revival week.

5. A large revival choir will be enlisted to sing each service.

6. Counselors will be enlisted and trained to assist in the invitations.

7. The Publicity Committee is responsible for advertising the revival to both members and the community.

Revival Week Schedule

Sunday: <u>Sunday School Unified Evangelistic Service</u> for grades 3-12 with evangelistic teaching "How to Be Saved and Know It."

Monday: <u>Sunday School Rally Night</u> each class or department (according to size of church) will seek to have its average Sunday School attendance present this evening.

Tuesday: <u>Youth Joy Explosion</u> one hour before revival service (don't call this "Youth Night" --- this is exclusive).

Wednesday: <u>Men and Women's Night</u>. Adults are responsible for building the attendance this evening. There will be a special fellowship after the service or perhaps an all church meal before the service.

Thursday: <u>Children's Corny Dog Supper</u> one hour before the revival service (don't call this "Children's Night").

Friday: <u>Family Night</u> when an all out effort is made to get families and relatives to attend and sit together.

CONSIDER THESE GOALS

1. Have the church in a state of spiritual revival when the revival week begins.

2. Involve as many people as possible in preparation.

3. Average as many people in week night revival services as you average in Sunday School attendance.

THE REVIVAL STEERING COMMITTEE

The Steering Committee is made up of the pastor, who is the General Chairman, the Revival Secretary, and chairmen of the various committees.

GENERAL CHAIRMAN: PASTOR — Be responsible for coordinating revival preparation with the Steering Committee.

ADULT CHAIRMAN: _____ — Be responsible for involving adults in the revival, especially on Wednesday when the adults are responsible for building attendance. An adult Sunday School worker should probably be chairman of this committee.

CHILDREN'S CHAIRMAN: _____ — Be responsible for Children's Corny Dog Supper on Thursday. A Sunday School children's worker probably should be chairman.

CONTACT CHAIRMAN: _____ — Be responsible for enlisting a telephone crew and for building attendance on Family Night, Friday evening of the revival week.

COUNSELOR CHAIRMAN: _____ — Be responsible with pastor for enlisting and training counselors to be used during invitations at revival services. <u>The pastor, especially of smaller churches, may want to assume this responsibility.</u>

MUSIC CHAIRMAN: _____ — Be responsible for enlisting a large revival choir to sing in each service. The minister of music or the music director probably should serve as chairman of this committee.

PRAYER CHAIRMAN: _____ — Be responsible for prayer preparation for revival. Select a prayer warrior who can get things done.

PUBLICITY CHAIRMAN: _____ — Be responsible for publicity of revival meeting.

REVIVAL SECRETARY: _____ — Assists the pastor in keeping everything on schedule and reproduces material for committee chairmen. The pastor's secretary or church secretary or a volunteer secretary might assume this reponsibility.

SUNDAY SCHOOL CHAIRMAN: _____ — Be responsible for Sunday School's part in revival preparation. The Sunday School director or minister of education probably should serve as this chairman.

VISITATION CHAIRMAN: Be responsible for enlisting visitation teams and coordinating visitation plans with pastor. The person responsible for church visitation probably should be chairman of this committee. <u>In churches with 150 or less, the pastor should probably be the chairman of this committee also.</u>

_____

YOUTH CHAIRMAN: Be responsible for youth visitation and the Youth Joy Explosion on Tuesday. The minister of youth or someone who works with youth in Sunday School would probably be the best chairman of this committee.

_____

STEERING COMMITTEE FOR SMALLER CHURCHES

General Chairman: Pastor (also serves as Visitation Chairman)

Prayer Chairman _____

Publicity Chairman _____

Sunday School Chairman _____

Contact Chairman _____

Then add as many of the other chairmen as you can:

_____   _____

_____   _____

_____   _____

_____   _____

_____   _____

CHAIRMAN TRAINING
Suggested Schedule

1:00 _____

1:30 _____

2:00 _____

2:30 _____

3:00 _____

3:30 _____

4:00 _____

4:30 _____

5:00 Dinner Break

5:30 _____

6:00 _____

6:30 _____

7:00 Combined Meeting - Steering Committee (6:30 or 7:30)

7:30 _____

8:00 _____

8:30 _____

It is usually best to use one afternoon and evening for this about seven to eight weeks before revival week. Sign up chairmen for thirty minutes each.

For those who cannot be trained at this time, set a date soon thereafter to train them.

Planning for Revival

General Chairman/Pastor

The pastor is the key to revival preparation. <u>In most cases he should serve as General Chairman</u>. In some cases, however, the pastor may want to assign the task to a staff member or enlist a well-qualified layman. <u>In any case, the pastor must stay close to the planning of a good revival</u>.

TEN WEEKS BEFORE THE REVIVAL:_____(dates)

1. Enlist all the committee chairmen. (See "The Revival Steering Committee", two and three pages prior to this one.) <u>Do not</u> give chairmen their materials at this time. Wait until time of training.

2. Schedule a day or two for orientation during Week VII before revival. Plan to spend 30 minutes with each chairman individually and then one 30-minute session with all chairmen together to show them how all the parts fit into one big plan. It is usually best to do this all in one day. For example: You might begin at 1:00 with one chairman, 1:30 with the next chairman, etc. Train those who work until 5:00 after that time and on into the evening. Then schedule 30 minutes that evening to bring all of the chairmen together at once. (See "Chairman Training Suggested Schedule", on the page prior to this one.)

SEVEN WEEKS BEFORE THE REVIVAL:_____(dates)

Conduct Chairman training as outlined above. <u>It is best that you wait until you train the chairman to give him his instruction materials</u>.

When training each chairman, first have him fill in the dates on his calendar as you should have filled them in on yours by this time. (You might want to fill in the dates yourself ahead of time.)

Then simply read through the instructions with each chairman. Make sure he knows three things: What he is to do, how he is to do it, and when he is to do it. Then try to motivate him to do his best. Be excited about what they are going to do, and help them to sense the importance of their jobs.

<u>PLEASE DON'T JUST GIVE THE INSTRUCTION MATERIALS TO THE CHAIRMEN AND TELL THEM TO DO WHAT IT SAYS.</u> Experience proves that it is definitely best to spend about 30 minutes going over the instructions with each chairman, answering any questions they might have and helping them to make any decisions necessary. <u>This training is extremely important</u>. Please give it your best, and your chairmen will usually reward you with their best.

At the conclusion of this training, bring all the chairmen together for about 30 minutes and show them how all the plans fit into one big plan. Tell who is going to be chairman of each committee and what his responsibilities are. (See "The Revival Steering Committee, two and three pages prior to this one.) Review "Brief Revival Overview." (This is located four pages prior to this one. Make copies to share.) This combined meeting is very important so please don't skip it. Prepare to make it the launching of a great revival.

COUNSELOR TRAINING

The pastor will work with the Counselor Chairman to enlist and train counselors. In smaller churches the pastor probably should assume the responsibility of this chairman. (See Counselor Chairman instructions.)

The pastor is responsible for training counselors. He should select the materials to be used in counseling. (See Chapter Ten, "Ideas on How To Prepare for Counseling".)

If someone other than the pastor is serving as General Chairman, then he must work this out with the pastor.

The rest of your instructions are contained in your countdown calendar on the following page.

General Chairman/Pastor Countdown Calendar

Week	Sunday	Monday	Tuesday	Wednesday	Thursday	Friday	Saturday
VI	Work with Visitation Chairman: (1) To prepare a list of people to enlist on visitation teams; (2) To begin plans to locate prospects (see Visitation Chairman instructions). Write to the revival evangelist and singer, share plans, request resumes and pictures (black and white glossies) for publicity. Ask the evangelist to send a letter on his stationery which can be sent to all the church members, or a copy of the letter which you can reproduce and send to all the church members.						
V	Talk to the Prayer Chairman about prayer events and personalities (see Prayer Chairman instructions).	Co-sign the letter with Visitation Chairman to be sent to those you hope to enlist on visitation teams. Also, complete plans to locate prospects (see Visitation Chairman instructions). Secure materials to be used to train counselors. (See instructions on front page.) Talk to Counselor Chairman about persons to enlist as counselors.					
IV		Work with Visitation Chairman to enlist visitation teams (see Visitation Chairman instructions.) Work with the Counselor Chairman to enlist counselors. (See Counselor Chairman instructions.) Work with church Hospitality Chairman (or selected lady) to plan the lodging and meals for the team during the revival week.					
III	Conduct STEERING COMMITTEE MEETING #1 (see Steering Committee Checklist on the following pages).		Work with Visitation Chairman in getting visitation assignments ready (see Visitation Chairman instructions). Write a letter to prospects. Ask the secretary to reproduce this letter and the letter from the evangelist to members. Both letters are to be mailed the week before the revival.				
II	Special prayer in a.m. and p.m. services (see Prayer Chairman instructions). Assist Visitation Chairman in Assignment Session #1 (see Visitation Chairman instructions). STEERING COMMITTEE #2	Participate in visitation to less active members (See Visitation Chm. instructions).		Conduct In-Church Cottage Prayer Meeting (see Prayer Chm.)			Teach Counselor Training
I	Special prayer in a.m. and p.m. services (see Prayer Chairman instructions). Assist Visitation Chairman in Assignment Session #2 (see Visitation Chm. instructions). STEERING COMMITTEE #3	Participate in visitation to prospects Mail letters from pastor		Conduct In-Church Cottage Prayer Meeting to prospects and from evangelist to members.	-------	-------	
REVIVAL	Sunday School Unified Evangelistic Service. (See Sunday School Chairman instructions.)	Sunday School Rally Night (see S.S. Chairman instructions).	Youth Joy Explosion one hour before service (see Youth Chm.)	All-Church dinner or after church fellowship (see Adult instrucions)	Children's Corny Dog Supper one hour before service (see Children's Chm.)	Family Night (see Contact Chairman)	Music Night if Saturday services (see Music Chm.)

Fill in revival dates then back up and fill in the other dates on the calendar. You will have a tailor-made countdown calendar for your committee.

Revival Preparation
Steering Committee Checklist

<u>How To Use</u>

Everything that any chairman is supposed to do is on the "Steering Committee Checklist", which serves as the Master Countdown Calendar. Fill in the dates in blanks.
Prior to the first Steering Committee Meeting, be sure to see that things are being done on schedule.
At each Steering Committee Meeting, the Pastor/General Chairman should review with the committee everything that should have been done up to that time and check off those things completed. Also, the Pastor/General Chairman reviews everything that is to be done the next week. Each chairman gives a progress report. Sometimes decisions are made. Always there should be a time for prayer.

WEEK VI: _____(dates)

_____ <u>Pastor/General Chairman</u>: Work with Visitation Chairman to enlist visitation teams and locate prospects.

_____ <u>Adult Chairman</u>: Enlist committee.

_____ <u>Children's Chairman</u>: Enlist committee. Enlist special feature for children's event.

_____ <u>Counselor Chairman</u>: Order materials. Talk to pastor about those to enlist for counselors.

_____ <u>Contact Chairman</u>: Enlist committee.

_____ <u>Music Chairman</u>: Write revival singer and share plans.

_____ <u>Prayer Chairman</u>: Enlist committee.

_____ <u>Publicity Chairman</u>: Enlist committee.

_____ <u>Youth Chairman</u>: Enlist Committee.

_____ <u>Visitation Chairman</u>: Enlist committee. See that letter is reproduced about visitation.

WEEK V: _____(dates)

_____ <u>Pastor/General Chairman</u>: Discuss prayer events with Prayer Chairman. Continue working with Visitation Chairman on enlisting visitation teams and locating prospects.

_____ <u>Music Chairman</u>: Enlist revival instrumentalists.

_____ <u>Prayer Chairman</u>: Discuss with pastor those to lead prayers during Sunday worship services of Weeks II and I. Also, discuss arrangements for In-Church Cottage prayer meetings. Prepare materials to promote daily prayer.

_____ <u>Publicity Chairman</u>: Write revival team and request biographical information and pictures. Check on yard sign.

_____ <u>Revival Secretary</u>: Help Prayer Chairman reproduce and order materials. Reproduce "I Know A Prospect" cards for Visitation Chairman. Put article in newsletter about revival dates, Steering Committee, etc.

_____ <u>Youth Chairman</u>: Enlist ladies to be responsible for meal for Youth Joy Explosion.

_____ <u>Visitation Chairman</u>: Mail letter and see that prospect cards are reproduced.

WEEK IV: _____(dates)

_____ <u>Pastor/General Chairman</u>: Work with Visitation Chairman to enlist teams. Work with Counselor Chairman to enlist counselors. Work with church hostess in planning meals and lodging for revival team.

WEEK IV: (continued)

    _____ Adult Chairman: Plan after-church fellowship.

    _____ Counselor Chairman: Enlist counselors.

    _____ Contact Chairman: Enlist Contact Crew.

    _____ Music Chairman: Prepare choir enlistment cards and memos.

    _____ Prayer Chairman: Meet with committee and make plans. Promote daily prayer in midweek service. Enlist people to lead special prayers during worship services.

    _____ Publicity Chairman: Prepare and print publicity materials. Enlist boys and girls to distribute circulars.

    _____ Revival Secretary: Help Music Chairman prepare choir enlistment cards and memo. Help Publicity Chairman prepare and print materials. Help Sunday School Chairman reproduce materials. Call Steering Committee members about meeting.

    _____ Sunday School Chairman: Meet with teachers and department directors and share plans. Prepare sign-up cards.

    _____ Youth Chairman: Enlist youth to serve on Youth Phone Crew.

    _____ Visitation Chairman: Conduct Inside Survey. Enlist visitors for visitation.

WEEK III:_____(dates)

    _____ Pastor/General Chairman: Work with Visitation Chairman in getting assignments ready. Write letter to prospects.

    _____ Adult Chairman: Enlist adults to make posters for Men & Women's Night.

    _____ Children's Chairman: Enlist ladies to prepare Corny Dog Supper.

    _____ Counselor Chairman: Be sure materials have been ordered.

    _____ Contact Chairman: Prepare assignments.

    _____ Music Chairman: Mail memo to all choir prospects.

    _____ Prayer Chairman: Have secretary put prayer reminder in church newsletter and bulletins.

    _____ Publicity Chairman: Put posters up in church buildings.

    _____ Revival Secretary: Reproduce memo and tickets for youth event. Reproduce and mail letter from evangelist to prospects. Put prayer reminder in church newsletter and Sunday bulletin. Call Steering Committee members about meeting.

    _____ Youth Chairman: See that memo and tickets are reproduced.

    _____ Visitation Chairman: Conclude Inside Survey. Prepare Visitation Assignment Cards.

WEEK II:_____(dates)

    _____ Pastor/General Chairman: Special prayer in worship services. Assist Visitation Chairman in Assignment Session #1. Conduct In-Church Cottage Prayer Meeting on Wednesday. Conduct Counselor Training.

    _____ Adult Chairman: Have the memo reproduced about Men & Women's Night.

    _____ Children's Chairman: Have tickets and memo for Corny Dog Supper reproduced. Ask children to make posters to advertise childrens events.

WEEK II: (continued)

____ Counselor Chairman: Call counselors about Counselor Training.

____ Contact Chairman: Have memos reproduced and mailed.

____ Music Chairman: Begin revival choir sign-up.

____ Prayer Chairman: Special prayer in worship services. In-Church Cottage Prayer meeting during midweek service.

____ Publicity Chairman: Put article in church newsletter about revival singer. Also, promote revival events. Put posters around town. Put yard sign up.

____ Revival Secretary: Help Adult Chairman reproduce memo. Help Children's Chairman reproduce memo and tickets. Help Contact Chairman reproduce memo and invitation cards. Put article in church newsletter about revival singer. Call Steering Committee members about meeting Sunday.

____ Sunday School Chairman: Pray for revival in Sunday School classes/departments. Meet with Sunday School teachers and officers and explain events. Distribute material.

____ Youth Chairman: Enlist youth to make posters to advertise youth events during revival. Prepare assignments for Youth Phone Crew.

____ Visitation Chairman: Promote visitation in Sunday School classes/departments. See that visitation is promoted in church bulletin and newsletter.

WEEK I: _____(dates)

____ Pastor/General Chairman: Special prayer in worship services. Assist in Visitation Assignment Session #2. Conduct In-Church Cottage Prayer Meeting.

____ Adult Chairman: Promote Men and Women's Night in Sunday School. Mail memos.

____ Children's Chairman: Promote Corny Dog Supper in Sunday School. Mail memo and tickets.

____ Contact Chairman: Committee and crew members address invitations to church and prospects. Contact crew make first telephone calls.

____ Music Chairman: Complete revival choir sign-up.

____ Prayer Chairman: Special prayer in worship services. In-Church Cottage Prayer meeting during midweek service.

____ Publicity Chairman: Put article in newsletter about revival preacher. Promote revival events. Send news release to newspaper about revival. Distribute circulars.

____ Revival Secretary: Put insert in bulletin with revival information. Mail letters from pastor to prospects. Help Contact Chairman get invitations addressed. Put article in church newsletter about revival preacher.

____ Sunday School Chairman: Pray for revival in Sunday School and promote Sunday School Rally Night. Prepare banners for Rally Night. Enlist and train counselors for United Evangelistic Service.

____ Youth Chairman: Prepare and mail memo and tickets. Mail telephone assignments to Youth Phone Crew.

____ Visitation Chairman: Steering Committee Meeting. Promote visitation in Sunday School classes/departments.

WEEK OF REVIVAL: _____(dates)

____ Pastor/General Chairman: Sunday School United Service. Promote High Attendance Day in Sunday School.

WEEK OF REVIVAL: (continued)

_____ Adult Chairman: Promote Men and Women's Night in Sunday School. Also, promote Sunday School Rally Night.

_____ Children's Chairman: Promote Corny Dog Supper in Sunday School. Sign-up children for Sunday School Rally Night. Finalize plans for corny dog supper.

_____ Counselor Chairman: Counselors assist in invitations.

_____ Contact Chairman: Call contact crew and remind them to make second calls. Mail invitations. Ask pastor to promote Family Night during revival services.

_____ Publicity Chairman: See that revival schedule is printed in bulletin.

_____ Revival Secretary: Put insert in bulletin with revival schedule.

_____ Sunday School Chairman: Continue signing up classes/departments for Rally Night.

_____ Youth Chairman: Promote youth events during Sunday School. Sign up youth for Sunday School Rally Night.

1. Keep one copy in the book.
2. Give one copy to chairmen.

Planning for Revival

Adult Chairman

This committee is responsible for the Men and Women's Night at the revival on Wednesday. Plan carefully for this special event.

During the revival service that evening you might have a popular guest personality share his/her Christian testimony. Talk to the pastor about inviting someone like a professional athlete, a high school or college coach, a musical group, an entertainer, etc. Use someone that the non-church-goer would want to come and hear. This will take money, but it will be worth it. Be sure to limit the guest's part in the service to 15 minutes. A longer time will take from the preaching and especially the invitation. Be sure your guest knows his time limit before he comes.

Plan an after-church fellowship. It could be a homemade ice cream feed, a talent show, or fun and games. You could have a men's cake bake contest, or a mock opera, etc. You might have a "Pastor's Roast." You might prefer a staff appreciation event or a "Queen-for-the-Day" for the pastor's wife. Whatever you do, be creative, and make it a most enjoyable event, especially for men and women.

You might prefer to have an all-church dinner before the service. If so, enlist a crew to prepare the meal.

Have the nursery workers care for the small children and babies during the fellowship.

Encourage the adults to invite their friends and neighbors to come with them to Men and Women's Night at the revival.

Also work with the revival Sunday School Chairman to promote Sunday School Rally Night on Monday evening of the revival week. Be sure adults are well represented.

Instructions for Reproducing Memo

On a separate page in the book you have a "Memo to Announce Men and Women's Night at the Revival." Be sure you have this. (Check with General Chairman.)

Fill in the church name and location, as well as the revival dates and time of services. Write your own message in the blank space in the middle of the page. Share your plans to make this a special night for adults. Make it sound exciting. Have copies made. This can be done on a copy machine or an offset press.

In smaller churches where there is no secretary, then type or handwrite the information. You might have copies made at a business, banks, schools, or other churches. <u>Ask the pastor for help with this if needed</u>.

Adult Chairman Countdown Calendar

Week	Sunday	Monday	Tuesday	Wednesday	Thursday	Friday	Saturday
VI		Enlist committee. Use adult Sunday School directors or teachers on the committee.					
V							
IV		Plan the after-church fellowship. (See instructions.)					
III	STEERING COMMITTEE MEETING: Be prepared to give progress report.		Ask some of the adults to make posters announcing Men and Women's Night at the revival. Display in adult Sunday School areas the Sunday before the revival and first Sunday of the revival.				
II	STEERING COMMITTEE MEETING: Be prepared to give progress report.		Ask the secretary to help reproduce the memo to adults about Men and Women's Night at the revival. (See sample.) Send to all adult members and prospects. The committee is to stuff, stamp, and address the letter. (Mail about Wednesday or Thursday of next week.)				
I	Promote Men & Women's Night at the Revival in adult Sunday School departments. STEERING COMMITTEE MEETING: Be prepared to give progress report.		Finalize plans for Men and Women's Night.		Mail memos to adults.		
REVIVAL	Promote Men and Women's Night in adult Sunday School departments. Also promote Sunday School Rally Night on Monday and have special prayer for revival.	SUNDAY SCHOOL RALLY NIGHT		MEN & WOMEN'S NIGHT AT THE REVIVAL			

Fill in revival dates then back up and fill in the other dates on the calendar. You will have a tailor-made countdown calendar for your committee.

1. Keep one copy in the book.
2. Give one copy to chairmen.

Planning for Revival

Adult Chairman

This committee is responsible for the Men and Women's Night at the revival on Wednesday. Plan carefully for this special event.

During the revival service that evening you might have a popular guest personality share his/her Christian testimony. Talk to the pastor about inviting someone like a professional athlete, a high school or college coach, a musical group, an entertainer, etc. Use someone that the non-church-goer would want to come and hear. This will take money, but it will be worth it. Be sure to limit the guest's part in the service to 15 minutes. A longer time will take from the preaching and especially the invitation. Be sure your guest knows his time limit before he comes.

Plan an after-church fellowship. It could be a homemade ice cream feed, a talent show, or fun and games. You could have a men's cake bake contest, or a mock opera, etc. You might have a "Pastor's Roast." You might prefer a staff appreciation event or a "Queen-for-the-Day" for the pastor's wife. Whatever you do, be creative, and make it a most enjoyable event, especially for men and women.

You might prefer to have an all-church dinner before the service. If so, enlist a crew to prepare the meal.

Have the nursery workers care for the small children and babies during the fellowship.

Encourage the adults to invite their friends and neighbors to come with them to Men and Women's Night at the revival.

Also work with the revival Sunday School Chairman to promote Sunday School Rally Night on Monday evening of the revival week. Be sure adults are well represented.

Instructions for Reproducing Memo

On a separate page in the book you have a "Memo to Announce Men and Women's Night at the Revival." Be sure you have this. (Check with General Chairman.)

Fill in the church name and location, as well as the revival dates and time of services. Write your own message in the blank space in the middle of the page. Share your plans to make this a special night for adults. Make it sound exciting. Have copies made. This can be done on a copy machine or an offset press.

In smaller churches where there is no secretary, then type or handwrite the information. You might have copies made at a business, banks, schools, or other churches. <u>Ask the pastor for help with this if needed</u>.

Adult Chairman Countdown Calendar

Week	Sunday	Monday	Tuesday	Wednesday	Thursday	Friday	Saturday
VI	Enlist committee. Use adult Sunday School directors or teachers on the committee.						
V							
IV	Plan the after-church fellowship. (See instructions.)						
III	STEERING COMMITTEE MEETING: Be prepared to give progress report.	Ask some of the adults to make posters announcing Men and Women's Night at the revival. Display in adult Sunday School areas the Sunday before the revival and first Sunday of the revival.					
II	STEERING COMMITTEE MEETING: Be prepared to give progress report.	Ask the secretary to help reproduce the memo to adults about Men and Women's Night at the revival. (See sample.) Send to all adult members and prospects. The committee is to stuff, stamp, and address the letter. (Mail about Wednesday or Thursday of next week.)					
I	Promote Men & Women's Night at the Revival in adult Sunday School departments. STEERING COMMITTEE MEETING: Be prepared to give progress report.	Finalize plans for Men and Women's Night.			Mail memos to adults.		
REVIVAL	Promote Men and Women's Night in adult Sunday School departments. Also promote Sunday School Rally Night on Monday and have special prayer for revival.	SUNDAY SCHOOL RALLY NIGHT		MEN & WOMEN'S NIGHT AT THE REVIVAL			

Fill in revival dates then back up and fill in the other dates on the calendar. You will have a tailor-made countdown calendar for your committee.

Memo to announce
Men and Women's Night at the Revival

Come be a part of an exciting special evening for adults and family.

_____
(Church and Location)

_____
(Revival Dates)   (Time)

1. Keep one copy in the book.
2. Give one copy to chairmen.

Planning for Revival

Children's Chairman

This committee is responsible for the Corny Dog Supper for children, grades one to six, to be held one hour before the revival service on Thursday (Wednesday of four day revivals). The program should be planned carefully. Here is a suggested schedule:

> 20 minutes for serving and eating
> 20 minutes for special feature
> 10 minutes for the evangelist
> 10 minutes to go to the restroom
> and get into the auditorium

Start serving the meal on time one hour before the service. Use several serving lines. Have several tables set-up and use both sides to serve. Have the food and drinks ready so the children can pick them up quickly.

After the meal have the blessing. Give each child a 3"x5" index card and pencil and have them write their name, address, telephone number, where they go to church, and how often. This should supply new prospects.

The special feature might be a puppet group, a magician, ventriloquist, clown, etc. The evangelist needs about 10 minutes to briefly and simply share the plan of salvation. No invitation is given at the Corny Dog Supper.

Reserve a section in the auditorium for children, usually on one side, at the front. You might ask children to sit with parents if they are present, especially first and second graders. <u>Have plenty of adults to sit among the children.</u> The revival service this evening should be shorter than usual.

<u>Do not</u> call this Children's Night. Many adults and youth might not attend thinking the service is for children.

Work with the revival Sunday School Chairman to promote Sunday School Rally Night on Monday evening of the revival week. Be sure children are well represented.

Check with the Revival Music Chairman about the children singing in the Friday evening revival service. He may want you to promote this at the Corny Dog Supper and even give out invitations. Friday is Family Night and many parents might come to hear their children sing.

Instructions for Reproducing Memo and Tickets

On a separate page in the book, you have a "Kids Announcement" memo and a page of tickets. Be sure you have these. (Check with General Chairman.)

To prepare the memo you need to type a note to the children in the center space; fill in the blanks at the bottom of the page, and reproduce. To prepare the tickets, simply fill in the blanks, reproduce, and cut apart. Ask the Revival Secretary to help with this.

If there is no Revival Secretary, type or handwrite the information. To reproduce these, they may be taken to a quick print shop or copies made on a copy machine. Many businesses such as banks, schools, or other churches have copy machines and will assist you with this. <u>You might ask the pastor to help.</u>

<u>Be sure to have the time the Corny Dog Supper begins and the revival service ends.</u> Example 6:30-8:45. The children may go home after the Corny Dog Supper unless you state beginning and ending times.

Children's Chairman Countdown Calendar

Week	Sunday	Monday	Tuesday	Wednesday	Thursday	Friday	Saturday
VI		Enlist other children's workers in Sunday School to be on your committee. Begin planning. Enlist a puppet group, magician, ventriloquist, clown, etc., to be the special feature at the Corny Dog Supper.					
V							
IV							
III	STEERING COMMITTEE MEETING: Be prepared to give progress report.	Enlist ladies to prepare Corny Dog Supper. Plan the meal carefully and keep the menu simple. Corny dogs, potato chips, and cold drinks. Corny dogs can be ordered from a food wholesaler or bought at a grocery store. Get the kind that are pre-cooked and need only to be reheated in an oven. Estimate number to attend and plan for a large crowd. Have plenty of adult help.					
II	Consider asking children to make posters to advertise the Corny Dog Supper. Put these up next Sunday. STEERING COMMITTEE MEETING: Be prepared to give progress report.	Ask the secretary to reproduce the memo and tickets to be mailed next week. See sample memo and tickets to be reproduced. You need a memo for each child, grades one through six, who is enrolled in Sunday School or is a prospect. Don't send brother's and sister's memos together. Each child received 5 tickets with his memo. Print extra tickets to give to children who want more. (See instructions for reproducing the memo and tickets on the front side of these instructions.)					
I	Promote Corny Dog Supper in Children' Sunday School department/classes. STEERING COMMITTEE MEETING: Be prepared to give progress report.	The committee is to stuff, stamp, and address the envelopes with memos and tickets to children.			Mail memos and tickets		
REVIVAL	Promote the Corny Dog Supper in Sunday School. Hand out extra tickets. Sign up children for Sunday School Rally Night on Monday evening of revival	Finalize plans for Corny Dog Supper. SUNDAY SCHOOL RALLY NIGHT			CHILDREN'S CORNY DOG SUPPER	(Children's Choir sing in service.)	

Fill in revival dates then back up and fill in the other dates on the calendar. You will have a tailor-made countdown calendar for your committee.

1. Keep one copy in the book.
2. Give one copy to chairmen.

Planning for Revival

Children's Chairman

This committee is responsible for the Corny Dog Supper for children, grades one to six, to be held one hour before the revival service on Thursday (Wednesday of four day revivals). The program should be planned carefully. Here is a suggested schedule:

> 20 minutes for serving and eating
> 20 minutes for special feature
> 10 minutes for the evangelist
> 10 minutes to go to the restroom
> and get into the auditorium

Start serving the meal on time one hour before the service. Use several serving lines. Have several tables set-up and use both sides to serve. Have the food and drinks ready so the children can pick them up quickly.

After the meal have the blessing. Give each child a 3"x5" index card and pencil and have them write their name, address, telephone number, where they go to church, and how often. This should supply new prospects.

The special feature might be a puppet group, a magician, ventriloquist, clown, etc. The evangelist needs about 10 minutes to briefly and simply share the plan of salvation. No invitation is given at the Corny Dog Supper.

Reserve a section in the auditorium for children, usually on one side, at the front. You might ask children to sit with parents if they are present, especially first and second graders. <u>Have plenty of adults to sit among the children.</u> The revival service this evening should be shorter than usual.

<u>Do not</u> call this Children's Night. Many adults and youth might not attend thinking the service is for children.

Work with the revival Sunday School Chairman to promote Sunday School Rally Night on Monday evening of the revival week. Be sure children are well represented.

Check with the Revival Music Chairman about the children singing in the Friday evening revival service. He may want you to promote this at the Corny Dog Supper and even give out invitations. Friday is Family Night and many parents might come to hear their children sing.

Instructions for Reproducing Memo and Tickets

On a separate page in the book, you have a "Kids Announcement" memo and a page of tickets. Be sure you have these. (Check with General Chairman.)

To prepare the memo you need to type a note to the children in the center space; fill in the blanks at the bottom of the page, and reproduce. To prepare the tickets, simply fill in the blanks, reproduce, and cut apart. Ask the Revival Secretary to help with this.

If there is no Revival Secretary, type or handwrite the information. To reproduce these, they may be taken to a quick print shop or copies made on a copy machine. Many businesses such as banks, schools, or other churches have copy machines and will assist you with this. <u>You might ask the pastor to help.</u>

<u>Be sure to have the time the Corny Dog Supper begins and the revival service ends.</u> Example 6:30-8:45. The children may go home after the Corny Dog Supper unless you state beginning and ending times.

Children's Chairman Countdown Calendar

Week	Sunday	Monday	Tuesday	Wednesday	Thursday	Friday	Saturday
VI		Enlist other children's workers in Sunday School to be on your committee. Begin planning. Enlist a puppet group, magician, ventriloquist, clown, etc., to be the special feature at the Corny Dog Supper.					
V							
IV							
III	STEERING COMMITTEE MEETING: Be prepared to give progress report.	Enlist ladies to prepare Corny Dog Supper. Plan the meal carefully and keep the menu simple. Corny dogs, potato chips, and cold drinks. Corny dogs can be ordered from a food wholesaler or bought at a grocery store. Get the kind that are pre-cooked and need only to be reheated in an oven. Estimate number to attend and plan for a large crowd. Have plenty of adult help.					
II	Consider asking children to make posters to advertise the Corny Dog Supper. Put these up next Sunday. STEERING COMMITTEE MEETING: Be prepared to give progress report.	Ask the secretary to reproduce the memo and tickets to be mailed next week. See sample memo and tickets to be reproduced. You need a memo for each child, grades one through six, who is enrolled in Sunday School or is a prospect. Don't send brother's and sister's memos together. Each child received 5 tickets with his memo. Print extra tickets to give to children who want more. (See instructions for reproducing the memo and tickets on the front side of these instructions.)					
I	Promote Corny Dog Supper in Children' Sunday School department/classes. STEERING COMMITTEE MEETING: Be prepared to give progress report.	The committee is to stuff, stamp, and address the envelopes with memos and tickets to children.			Mail memos and tickets		
REVIVAL	Promote the Corny Dog Supper in Sunday School. Hand out extra tickets. Sign up children for Sunday School Rally Night on Monday evening of revival	Finalize plans for Corny Dog Supper. SUNDAY SCHOOL RALLY NIGHT			CHILDREN'S CORNY DOG SUPPER	(Children's Choir sing in service.)	

Fill in revival dates then back up and fill in the other dates on the calendar. You will have a tailor-made countdown calendar for your committee.

Kid's Announcement

 ## Corny Dog Supper for grades 1-6

Round up your friends and the kids in your
neighborhood and come to the big Corny Dog Supper.

_____
(church and location)

_____
(revival dates and time of services)

ADMIT TWO
Corny Dog Supper

_____ _____ _____
Date   Day   Time
_____
Church
_____
Address

_____
Special Feature

ADMIT TWO
Corny Dog Supper

_____ _____ _____
Date   Day   Time
_____
Church
_____
Address

_____
Special Feature

ADMIT TWO
Corny Dog Supper

_____ _____ _____
Date   Day   Time
_____
Church
_____
Address

_____
Special Feature

ADMIT TWO
Corny Dog Supper

_____ _____ _____
Date   Day   Time
_____
Church
_____
Address

_____
Special Feature

ADMIT TWO
Corny Dog Supper

_____ _____ _____
Date   Day   Time
_____
Church
_____
Address

_____
Special Feature

ADMIT TWO
Corny Dog Supper

_____ _____ _____
Date   Day   Time
_____
Church
_____
Address

_____
Special Feature

1. Keep one copy in the book.
2. Give one copy to chairmen.

Planning for Revival

Contact Chairman

This committee is responsible for two things: (1) telephoning all the church families and prospects before the revival week; (2) helping build the attendance for Family Night on Friday by a written invitation and a second telephone call to all the church families and prospects.

Ask the church secretary, minister of education or pastor to help you determine the number of church families as well as the number of prospective families. If only one family member belongs to the church, consider this a family. Remember, the rest of the family are prospects.

        Church families   _____ (number)

        Prospective families   _____ (number)

        TOTAL families to contact   _____

On Family Night you might want to have special recognition for the family with the most relatives present and/or let families introduce relatives who are guests. For example, ask children to introduce grandparents.

Instructions for Reproducing Memo and Invitation Cards

On a separate page in the book you have two pieces of art work, "Memo to Revival Contact Crew" and "Family Night at the Revival" invitation cards. Be sure you have these. (Check with the General Chairman.)

The memo is ready to reproduce as is or you may want to rewrite it. Put your name beside "Contact Chairman." To reproduce the invitation cards, fill in the information needed. Make copies, and cut cards apart. These must be on card stock for mailing. Ask the Revival Secretary to help with this.

If there is no Revival Secretary, type or handwrite the information on cards. To reproduce, you might take them to a quick print shop, or have copies made on a copy machine. Many banks, schools, or other churches have copy machines and may help you with this. One way or another, you can do it. <u>Ask the pastor to help</u>.

Contact Chairman Countdown Calendar

Week	Sunday	Monday	Tuesday	Wednesday	Thursday	Friday	Saturday
VI	Enlist committee. If you have less than 150 families (members and prospects) to contact, your Contact Crew will be your committee. If you have more than 150 families (members and prospects) to contact, you need one committee member for every 150 families to be contacted. Enlist one or two from each adult Sunday School department.						
V							
IV	Enlist Contact Crew. Each committee member enlists 10 people from his/her Adult Sunday School department to serve on the Contact Crew. Each Contact Crew member will be responsible for contacting 15 families (members and prospects). In churches with less than 150 families, enlist one crew member for each 15 families to be contacted.						
III	STEERING COMMITTEE MEETING: Be prepared to give progress report.		Prepare assignments. Put 15 names of church families and prospects to be contacted on each page. Give each caller an equal number of church families and prospective families to call. Then assign each page of 15 families to be contacted to a Contact Crew member.				
II	STEERING COMMITTEE MEETING: Be prepared to give progress report.		Ask the secretary to help reproduce the memo, with instructions and the invitation cards (see samples). The committee is to address, stuff, stamp, and mail the memo by Friday. (See instructions for reproducing these materials on the front page of these instructions.) Be sure to send a page about the evangelistic team and revival events with the memo; also include a list of families and telephone numbers.				
I	STEERING COMMITTEE MEETING: Be prepared to give progress report.				Contact Crew make first telephone calls to all those assigned to them. Contact committee and crew members address invitations to church and prospective families. (Many churches have addressing machines and can be used for members. Ask secretary about this.) Mail these on Monday of the revival week. Don't mail too early.		
REVIVAL	Call all Contact Crew and remind to make second calls. Ask the pastor to promote Family Night during each revival service.	Mail Invitations	Contact crew make second telephone calls to those assigned to them.			FAMILY NIGHT	

Fill in revival dates then back up and fill in the other dates on the calendar. You will have a tailor-made countdown calendar for your committee.

1. Keep one copy in the book.
2. Give one copy to chairmen.

Planning for Revival

Contact Chairman

This committee is responsible for two things: (1) telephoning all the church families and prospects before the revival week; (2) helping build the attendance for Family Night on Friday by a written invitation and a second telephone call to all the church families and prospects.

Ask the church secretary, minister of education or pastor to help you determine the number of church families as well as the number of prospective families. If only one family member belongs to the church, consider this a family. Remember, the rest of the family are prospects.

        Church families   _____ (number)

        Prospective families   _____ (number)

        TOTAL families to contact   _____

On Family Night you might want to have special recognition for the family with the most relatives present and/or let families introduce relatives who are guests. For example, ask children to introduce grandparents.

Instructions for Reproducing Memo and Invitation Cards

On a separate page in the book you have two pieces of art work, "Memo to Revival Contact Crew" and "Family Night at the Revival" invitation cards. Be sure you have these. (Check with the General Chairman.)

The memo is ready to reproduce as is or you may want to rewrite it.. Put your name beside "Contact Chairman." To reproduce the invitation cards, fill in the information needed. Make copies, and cut cards apart. These must be on card stock for mailing. Ask the Revival Secretary to help with this.

If there is no Revival Secretary, type or handwrite the information on cards. To reproduce, you might take them to a quick print shop, or have copies made on a copy machine. Many banks, schools, or other churches have copy machines and may help you with this. One way or another, you can do it. <u>Ask the pastor to help</u>.

Contact Chairman Countdown Calendar

Week	Sunday	Monday	Tuesday	Wednesday	Thursday	Friday	Saturday
VI	Enlist committee. If you have less than 150 families (members and prospects) to contact, your Contact Crew will be your committee. If you have more than 150 families (members and prospects) to contact, you need one committee member for every 150 families to be contacted. Enlist one or two from each adult Sunday School department.						
V							
IV	Enlist Contact Crew. Each committee member enlists 10 people from his/her Adult Sunday School department to serve on the Contact Crew. Each Contact Crew member will be responsible for contacting 15 families (members and prospects). In churches with less than 150 families, enlist one crew member for each 15 families to be contacted.						
III	STEERING COMMITTEE MEETING: Be prepared to give progress report.	Prepare assignments. Put 15 names of church families and prospects to be contacted on each page. Give each caller an equal number of church families and prospective families to call. Then assign each page of 15 families to be contacted to a Contact Crew member.					
II	STEERING COMMITTEE MEETING: Be prepared to give progress report.	Ask the secretary to help reproduce the memo, with instructions and the invitation cards (see samples). The committee is to address, stuff, stamp, and mail the memo by Friday. (See instructions for reproducing these materials on the front page of these instructions.) Be sure to send a page about the evangelistic team and revival events with the memo; also include a list of families and telephone numbers.					
I	STEERING COMMITTEE MEETING: Be prepared to give progress report.	Contact committee and crew members address invitations to church and prospective families. (Many churches have addressing machines and can be used for members. Ask secretary about this.) Mail these on Monday of the revival week. Don't mail too early.			Contact Crew make first telephone calls to all those assigned to them.		
REVIVAL	Call all Contact Crew and remind to make second calls. Ask the pastor to promote Family Night during each revival service.	Mail Invitations	Contact crew make second telephone calls to those assigned to them.			FAMILY NIGHT	

Fill in revival dates then back up and fill in the other dates on the calendar. You will have a tailor-made countdown calendar for your committee.

Planning for Revival

MEMORANDUM

TO: Revival Contact Crew

FROM: Contact Chairman, _____

I want to thank you for joining the Contact Crew. Enclosed is a list of those you are to contact. Also enclosed is information about the revival -- evangelists, date, time, etc.

Please call the families on Wednesday through Saturday of the week before our revival. Tell them about our coming revival, the evangelistic team, special events planned, etc.

Then call a second time on Tuesday, Wednesday, and Thursday of the revival week. Report to them the progress of the revival. Be enthusiastic. Then invite them to attend Family Night on Friday. Encourage them to bring their relatives who live in the area. Suggest that they might plan a family meal and then go to the Family Night service together.

Family Night At The Revival

Friday _____ at _____
            (date)   (time)

Families are encouraged to come and sit together for the Friday evening revival service. Invite your relatives who live in the area to come and sit with you.

_____   _____
Church   Location

Family Night At The Revival

Friday _____ at _____
            (date)   (time)

Families are encouraged to come and sit together for the Friday evening revival service. Invite your relatives who live in the area to come and sit with you.

_____   _____
Church   Location

Family Night At The Revival

Friday _____ at _____
            (date)   (time)

Families are encouraged to come and sit together for the Friday evening revival service. Invite your relatives who live in the area to come and sit with you.

_____   _____
Church   Location

Family Night At The Revival

Friday _____ at _____
            (date)   (time)

Families are encouraged to come and sit together for the Friday evening revival service. Invite your relatives who live in the area to come and sit with you.

_____   _____
Church   Location

1. Keep one copy in the book.
2. Give one copy to chairmen.

Planning for Revival

Counselor Chairman

The Counselor Committee is responsible for working with the pastor to enlist and train counselors who will assist those who come forward during the invitations at the revival service. In some churches, especially smaller ones, the pastor may serve as chairman of this committee.

Every person who comes forward, especially for salvation, needs a trained counselor to help him with his decision. If several people come during the invitation, the pastor will be unable to give each one the needed attention or else he will draw out the invitation much too long. Plus the fact that when the line starts forming to talk to the pastor, the people stop coming. Therefore, the pastor should have trained lay persons to assist him with this. Besides, this is a great opportunity for these people to become involved in soul-winning.

COUNSELORS NEEDED

Churches with 100 or less in average attendance need a minimum of 3 men and 3 women. Add 1-2 men and 1-2 women for each additional 100 average in attendance. In some cases where you expect an unusually large number to respond to the invitation, enlist more. Most counselors are also going to be on visitation teams, but this should not be an overload. Consider using these trained counselors each Sunday, even when you are not in a revival meeting.

COUNSELOR TRAINING

The pastor should conduct the counselor training. For this he has suggestions in the chapter on counseling in the book from which these chairman instructions were taken. Work out training procedures with him.

COUNSELING DURING INVITATION

The pastor (and staff) receives the inquirers as they come forward, hearing their decisions. He then motions for a counselor to assist the inquirer. The counseling may take place on a front pew immediately. Another way is to move to a counseling room and conduct counseling there. Where there are large numbers responding to the invitation, this might be the best way. Those desiring baptism and membership would then be recognized at a later service.

FOLLOW-UP COUNSELING

The pastor should visit later and counsel with everyone of those who made professions of faith and are candidates for baptism. Counselors, however, can be used to follow-up with the new converts.

COUNSELING MATERIALS

The pastor is responsible for securing materials for counseling. Talk to him about this. Offer to assist. (There is a chapter in the book from which these instructions were taken that deals with counselor training and materials.)

Counselor Chairman Countdown Calendar

Week	Sunday	Monday	Tuesday	Wednesday	Thursday	Friday	Saturday
VI							
V			Talk to pastor about persons to enlist as counselors. Offer to assist him in securing materials for counselor training.				
IV		Enlist counselors. areas for revival	Serving as a counselor will not interfere with serving in other preparation.				
III	STEERING COMMITTEE MEETING: Be prepared to give progress report.		Be sure counseling materials have been secured by ordering or reproducing.				
II	STEERING COMMITTEE MEETING: Be prepared to give progress report.				Call all the counselors and remind them to attend the counselor training. Don't omit this or some of your counselors will forget it.		COUNSELOR TRAINING
I	STEERING COMMITTEE MEETING: Be prepared to give progress report.						
REVIVAL	Counselors assist in invitations ----------			----------		----------	

Fill in revival dates then back up and fill in the other dates on the calendar. You will have a tailor-made countdown calendar for your committee.

1. Keep one copy in the book.
2. Give one copy to chairmen.

Planning for Revival

Counselor Chairman

The Counselor Committee is responsible for working with the pastor to enlist and train counselors who will assist those who come forward during the invitations at the revival service. In some churches, especially smaller ones, the pastor may serve as chairman of this committee.

Every person who comes forward, especially for salvation, needs a trained counselor to help him with his decision. If several people come during the invitation, the pastor will be unable to give each one the needed attention or else he will draw out the invitation much too long. Plus the fact that <u>when the line starts forming to talk to the pastor, the people stop coming</u>. Therefore, the pastor should have trained lay persons to assist him with this. Besides, this is a great opportunity for these people to become involved in soul-winning.

COUNSELORS NEEDED

Churches with 100 or less in average attendance need a minimum of 3 men and 3 women. Add 1-2 men and 1-2 women for each additional 100 average in attendance. In some cases where you expect an unusually large number to respond to the invitation, enlist more. Most counselors are also going to be on visitation teams, but this should not be an overload. Consider using these trained counselors each Sunday, even when you are not in a revival meeting.

COUNSELOR TRAINING

The pastor should conduct the counselor training. For this he has suggestions in the chapter on counseling in the book from which these chairman instructions were taken. Work out training procedures with him.

COUNSELING DURING INVITATION

The pastor (and staff) receives the inquirers as they come forward, hearing their decisions. He then motions for a counselor to assist the inquirer. The counseling may take place on a front pew immediately. Another way is to move to a counseling room and conduct counseling there. Where there are large numbers responding to the invitation, this might be the best way. Those desiring baptism and membership would then be recognized at a later service.

FOLLOW-UP COUNSELING

The pastor should visit later and counsel with everyone of those who made professions of faith and are candidates for baptism. Counselors, however, can be used to follow-up with the new converts.

COUNSELING MATERIALS

The pastor is responsible for securing materials for counseling. Talk to him about this. Offer to assist. (There is a chapter in the book from which these instructions were taken that deals with counselor training and materials.)

Counselor Chairman Countdown Calendar

Week	Sunday	Monday	Tuesday	Wednesday	Thursday	Friday	Saturday
VI							
V			Talk to pastor about persons to enlist as counselors. Offer to assist him in securing materials for counselor training.				
IV		Enlist counselors. areas for revival	Serving as a counselor will not interfere with serving in other preparation.				
III	STEERING COMMITTEE MEETING: Be prepared to give progress report.		Be sure counseling materials have been secured by ordering or reproducing.				
II	STEERING COMMITTEE MEETING: Be prepared to give progress report.				Call all the counselors and remind them to attend the counselor training. Don't omit this or some of your counselors will forget it.		COUNSELOR TRAINING
I	STEERING COMMITTEE MEETING: Be prepared to give progress report.						
REVIVAL	Counselors assist in invitations	----	----	----	----	----	----

Fill in revival dates then back up and fill in the other dates on the calendar. You will have a tailor-made countdown calendar for your committee.

1. Keep one copy in the book.
2. Give one copy to chairmen.

Planning for Revival

Music Chairman

This committee will be responsible for enlisting the revival choir and instrumentalists and assisting the revival singer in preparation for the revival music. The minister of music (or choir president) would be a good chairman for this work.

Set a goal to have the choir loft filled each evening and work hard to do it. It is extremely important, plus it might be a good time to enlist some new folks for your regular choir. Consideration should be given to inviting the older youth to sing in the revival choir.

If there is a Saturday night service, which most churches choose not to have, then it should be "Music Night." There might be a mini-concert by the guest music evangelist if he is a skilled soloist. You might use ensembles, quartets, trios, duets, or soloists in your church or invite guests from other churches. Perhpas, the congregation could request the hymns they would like to sing. Whatever you choose to do, do it well. Saturday night is a most difficult night to build a good attendance, so work hard to make it extremely attractive.

Instructions for Reproducing Memo and Cards

On a separate page in the book you have a "Revival Choir Memo" and "Revival Choir Enlistment Card." Be sure you have these. (Check with General Chairman.)

The memo is ready to reproduce as is or you may want to rewrite it. Put your name above "Music Chairman."

To reproduce the enlistment cards, cut the paper off, fill in the information needed, make copies, and cut apart. These need to be on card stock if possible. Ask the Revival Secretary to assist with this.

If there is no Revival Secretary, type or handwrite the information on the cards and memos. To reproduce, take them to a quick print shop or use a copy machine. Many banks, schools, or other churches might help you. One way or another, you can do it. <u>Ask your pastor to help.</u>

Music Chairman Countdown Calendar

Week	Sunday	Monday	Tuesday	Wednesday	Thursday	Friday	Saturday
VI		Write to revival singer and share plans. Ask for suggestions. Enlist committee.					
V		Enlist revival instrumentalists. Be ready to have competent pianists (and organists) for each revival service. They need to be able to play difficult music on fairly short notice. Consider inviting outside instrumentalists, if necessary.					
IV		Prepare choir enlistment cards and memo to prospective choir participants. (See instructions on front page.)					
III	STEERING COMMITTEE MEETING: Be prepared to give progress report.	Mail the memo to all prospective revival choir participants. The committee is to stuff, stamp, address, and mail the memo. Mail the memo to as many folks as you think might respond. Remember, a good, large choir is extremely important to a successful revival.					
II	STEERING COMMITTEE MEETING: Be prepared to give progress report.	Begin sign-up for revival choir. At choir rehearsals, have the members sign a "Revival Choir Enlistment Card" indicating what nights they plan to participate. Then assign those who sign up the names of people they might be able to sign up. Call all those to whom you sent memos who are not yet sign up. Work hard at this.					
I	STEERING COMMITTEE MEETING: Be prepared to give progress report.	Complete sign-up of revival choir. Be sure you have a good choir enlisted for each revival service.					
REVIVAL		Meet the choir 30 minutes before each evening service. Start the rehearsal on time and be prepared to start the revival service on time. See that the revival choir is used. The best way to kill a revival choir is for them not to sing in the services.					MUSIC NIGHT (if having Saturday evening services)

Fill in revival dates then back up and fill in the other dates on the calendar. You will have a tailor-made countdown calendar for your committee.

1. Keep one copy in the book.
2. Give one copy to chairmen.

Planning for Revival

Music Chairman

This committee will be responsible for enlisting the revival choir and instrumentalists and assisting the revival singer in preparation for the revival music. The minister of music (or choir president) would be a good chairman for this work.

Set a goal to have the choir loft filled each evening and work hard to do it. It is extremely important, plus it might be a good time to enlist some new folks for your regular choir. Consideration should be given to inviting the older youth to sing in the revival choir.

If there is a Saturday night service, which most churches choose not to have, then it should be "Music Night." There might be a mini-concert by the guest music evangelist if he is a skilled soloist. You might use ensembles, quartets, trios, duets, or soloists in your church or invite guests from other churches. Perhpas, the congregation could request the hymns they would like to sing. Whatever you choose to do, do it well. Saturday night is a most difficult night to build a good attendance, so work hard to make it extremely attractive.

Instructions for Reproducing Memo and Cards

On a separate page in the book you have a "Revival Choir Memo" and "Revival Choir Enlistment Card." Be sure you have these. (Check with General Chairman.)

The memo is ready to reproduce as is or you may want to rewrite it. Put your name above "Music Chairman."

To reproduce the enlistment cards, cut the paper off, fill in the information needed, make copies, and cut apart. These need to be on card stock if possible. Ask the Revival Secretary to assist with this.

If there is no Revival Secretary, type or handwrite the information on the cards and memos. To reproduce, take them to a quick print shop or use a copy machine. Many banks, schools, or other churches might help you. One way or another, you can do it. <u>Ask your pastor to help</u>.

Music Chairman Countdown Calendar

Week	Sunday	Monday	Tuesday	Wednesday	Thursday	Friday	Saturday
VI		Write to revival singer and share plans. Ask for suggestions. Enlist committee.					
V		Enlist revival instrumentalists. Be ready to have competent pianists (and organists) for each revival service. They need to be able to play difficult music on fairly short notice. Consider inviting outside instrumentalists, if necessary.					
IV		Prepare choir enlistment cards and memo to prospective choir participants. (See instructions on front page.)					
III	STEERING COMMITTEE MEETING: Be prepared to give progress report.	Mail the memo to all prospective revival choir participants. The committee is to stuff, stamp, address, and mail the memo. Mail the memo to as many folks as you think might respond. Remember, a good, large choir is extremely important to a successful revival.					
II	STEERING COMMITTEE MEETING: Be prepared to give progress report.	Begin sign-up for revival choir. At choir rehearsals, have the members sign a "Revival Choir Enlistment Card" indicating what nights they plan to participate. Then assign those who sign up the names of people they might be able to sign up. Call all those to whom you sent memos who are not yet sign up. Work hard at this.					
I	Complete sign-up of revival choir. Be sure you have a good choir enlisted for each revival service. STEERING COMMITTEE MEETING: Be prepared to give progress report.						
REVIVAL		Meet the choir 30 minutes before each evening service. Start the rehearsal on time and be prepared to start the revival service on time. See that the revival choir is used. The best way to kill a revival choir is for them not to sing in the services.					MUSIC NIGHT (if having Saturday evening services)

Fill in revival dates then back up and fill in the other dates on the calendar. You will have a tailor-made countdown calendar for your committee.

Revival Choir Memo from Revival Music Committee

    A good choir is very important to a good revival meeting. Therefore, I am asking you to sing in our revival choir.

    Please sign the enclosed choir card and turn it into me. Thank you for your consideration of this important matter.

    We will rehearse at _____(time) each evening during the revival week.

(chairman)

(church)

(revival dates and time of services)

TOGETHER WE SING

Realizing the importance of music in a revival, I will be present for the rehearsal and the service on the dates which I have circled, unless providentially hindered.

Date of Revival _____

SUN. MON. TUES. WED. THURS. FRI. SUN.

NAME _____ PHONE _____

ADDRESS _____

"Singing with grace in your hearts" (Col. 3:16)

TOGETHER WE SING

Realizing the importance of music in a revival, I will be present for the rehearsal and the service on the dates which I have circled, unless providentially hindered.

Date of Revival _____

SUN. MON. TUES. WED. THURS. FRI. SUN.

NAME _____ PHONE _____

ADDRESS _____

"Singing with grace in your hearts" (Col. 3:16)

TOGETHER WE SING

Realizing the importance of music in a revival, I will be present for the rehearsal and the service on the dates which I have circled, unless providentially hindered.

Date of Revival _____

SUN. MON. TUES. WED. THURS. FRI. SUN.

NAME _____ PHONE _____

ADDRESS _____

"Singing with grace in your hearts" (Col. 3:16)

TOGETHER WE SING

Realizing the importance of music in a revival, I will be present for the rehearsal and the service on the dates which I have circled, unless providentially hindered.

Date of Revival _____

SUN. MON. TUES. WED. THURS. FRI. SUN.

NAME _____ PHONE _____

ADDRESS _____

"Singing with grace in your hearts" (Col. 3:16)

1. Keep one copy in the book.
2. Give one copy to chairmen.

Planning for Revival

Prayer Chairman

The Prayer Chairman and his committee are responsible for the following:

1. Promoting daily prayer for revival --- both individual and family prayer. This will be done during morning or evening worship services on Sunday of Week III. Give each person present a "Prayer Commitment Card." Ask those present to commit themselves to pray for revival by signing the commitment card and returning it at this time. Also, give every person a "Remember to Pray for Our Revival" card and put it in some conspicuous place that will remind them to pray daily for the revival. Also, give each family a "Family Prayer for Revival" card which they will set up on their meal table to remind them to pray for the revival when they say the blessing at meal time. Repeat this a second week for those not present the first time.

2. <u>Special prayer for revival during Sunday morning and evening worship services of Weeks II and I.</u> In consultation with the pastor enlist four people to lead these prayers, one in each service. You may want them to share a testimony of their conversion (five minutes maximum time).

3. <u>In-Church Cottage Prayer Meeting on Wednesdays of Weeks II and I</u> (option: only Wednesday of Week I). Meet together for a brief word from the pastor and then break up into smaller groups by Sunday School departments and/or classes. The Sunday School representative on the Prayer Committee, or the Sunday School Director or class teacher might be the leader for these small prayer groups. See that each leader of a small group is given the following guidelines:

    (1) First read II Chronicles 7:14.
    (2) Pray for the church to experience spiritual revival.
    (3) Pray for the evangelistic team.
    (4) Ask for prayer requests and have someone to voice a short prayer after each individual request.

4. <u>Organizational Prayer</u>. Three to four weeks before the revival week, get every organization to have a special prayer for revival some time during every meeting.

COMMITTEE

Sunday School representatives on the Prayer Committee have a three-fold responsibility: (1) Encourage special prayer for revival in Sunday School departments and classes, especially on Sundays of Weeks II, I and the first Sunday of the revival; (2) Promote attendance at the In-Church Cottage Prayer meetings on Wednesdays of Weeks II and I. These representatives might also serve as the leaders of their departments or classes at the cottage prayer meeting; (3) Encourage department and class members to pray daily for the revival.

Organizational representatives on the Prayer Committee are responsible for encouraging their organizations to be sure to have special prayer for the revival every time they meet and to encourage daily prayer for the revival.

Instructions for Reproducing Prayer Materials

On a separate page in the manual you have some art work for cards that need to be reproduced. Be sure to secure these. (Check with General Chairman.)

To reproduce the cards type in or have information typeset --- dates, evangelist, etc. Ask the secretary to help with this. <u>Use card stock.</u>

If there is no Revival Secretary, then you might have a quick print shop to reproduce these for you. Copies might be made on copy machines that take card stock. <u>Ask your pastor to help with this.</u>

Prayer Chairman Countdown Calendar

Week	Sunday	Monday	Tuesday	Wednesday	Thursday	Friday	Saturday
VI			Enlist prayer committee: Sunday School department (or class) and one representative from such organizations as Deacon Body, W.M.U., Church Training, and others who meet regularly. Enlist one representative for each adult-youth				
V	Talk to pastor about people to lead special prayers for revival during Sunday worship services of Weeks II and I. Also discuss arrangements for In-Church Cottage Prayer Meetings.		Prepare materials needed to promote daily prayer for revival. (See instructions on front page.)				
IV	Meet with Prayer Committee, train representatives, and make plans. (See instructions on front page.)				Enlist people to lead special prayers during worship services of Weeks II and I.		
III	Ask the pastor to give you time in the a.m. or p.m. service to promote daily prayer for revival. STEERING COMMITTEE MEETING: Be prepared to give progress report.		Ask the secretary to put a prayer reminder for revival in all church mail outs and bulletins.				
II	Special prayer for revival during a.m. and p.m. worship services. (See instructions on page 1.) STEERING COMMITTEE MEETING: Be prepared to give progress report.			In-Church Cottage Prayer Mtgs. during mid-week service. (Optional) See instructions page 1.			
I	Special prayer for revival during a.m. and p.m. worship services. (See instructions on page 1.) STEERING COMMITTEE MEETING: Be prepared to give progress report.			In-Church Cottage Prayer Mtgs. during mid-week service. (See instructions page 1.)			
REVIVAL							

Fill in revival dates then back up and fill in the other dates on the calendar. You will have a tailor-made countdown calendar for your committee.

1. Keep one copy in the book.
2. Give one copy to chairmen.

Planning for Revival

Prayer Chairman

The Prayer Chairman and his committee are responsible for the following:

1. Promoting daily prayer for revival --- both individual and family prayer. This will be done during morning or evening worship services on Sunday of Week III. Give each person present a "Prayer Commitment Card." Ask those present to commit themselves to pray for revival by signing the commitment card and returning it at this time. Also, give every person a "Remember to Pray for Our Revival" card and put it in some conspicuous place that will remind them to pray daily for the revival. Also, give each family a "Family Prayer for Revival" card which they will set up on their meal table to remind them to pray for the revival when they say the blessing at meal time. Repeat this a second week for those not present the first time.

2. Special prayer for revival during Sunday morning and evening worship services of Weeks II and I. In consultation with the pastor enlist four people to lead these prayers, one in each service. You may want them to share a testimony of their conversion (five minutes maximum time).

3. In-Church Cottage Prayer Meeting on Wednesdays of Weeks II and I (option: only Wednesday of Week I). Meet together for a brief word from the pastor and then break up into smaller groups by Sunday School departments and/or classes. The Sunday School representative on the Prayer Committee, or the Sunday School Director or class teacher might be the leader for these small prayer groups. See that each leader of a small group is given the following guidelines:

    (1) First read II Chronicles 7:14.
    (2) Pray for the church to experience spiritual revival.
    (3) Pray for the evangelistic team.
    (4) Ask for prayer requests and have someone to voice a short prayer after each individual request.

4. Organizational Prayer. Three to four weeks before the revival week, get every organization to have a special prayer for revival some time during every meeting.

COMMITTEE

Sunday School representatives on the Prayer Committee have a three-fold responsibility: (1) Encourage special prayer for revival in Sunday School departments and classes, especially on Sundays of Weeks II, I and the first Sunday of the revival; (2) Promote attendance at the In-Church Cottage Prayer meetings on Wednesdays of Weeks II and I. These representatives might also serve as the leaders of their departments or classes at the cottage prayer meeting; (3) Encourage department and class members to pray daily for the revival.

Organizational representatives on the Prayer Committee are responsible for encouraging their organizations to be sure to have special prayer for the revival every time they meet and to encourage daily prayer for the revival.

Instructions for Reproducing Prayer Materials

On a separate page in the manual you have some art work for cards that need to be reproduced. Be sure to secure these. (Check with General Chairman.)

To reproduce the cards type in or have information typeset --- dates, evangelist, etc. Ask the secretary to help with this. Use card stock.

If there is no Revival Secretary, then you might have a quick print shop to reproduce these for you. Copies might be made on copy machines that take card stock. Ask your pastor to help with this.

Prayer Chairman Countdown Calendar

Week	Sunday	Monday	Tuesday	Wednesday	Thursday	Friday	Saturday
VI			Enlist prayer committee: Sunday School department (or class) and organizations as Deacon Body, W.M.U., meet regularly.	Enlist one representative for each adult-youth one representative from such Church Training, and others who			
V	Talk to pastor about people to lead special prayers for revival during Sunday worship services of Weeks II and I. Also discuss arrangements for In-Church Cottage Prayer Meetings.		Prepare materials needed to promote daily prayer for revival. (See instructions on front page.)				
IV	Meet with Prayer Committee, train representatives, and make plans. (See instructions on front page.)				Enlist people to lead special prayers during worship services of Weeks II and I.		
III	Ask the pastor to give you time in the a.m. or p.m. service to promote daily prayer for revival. STEERING COMMITTEE MEETING: Be prepared to give progress report.		Ask the secretary to put a prayer reminder for revival in all church mail outs and bulletins.				
II	Special prayer for revival during a.m. and p.m. worship services. (See instructions on page 1.) STEERING COMMITTEE MEETING: Be prepared to give progress report.			In-Church Cottage Prayer Mtgs. during midweek service. (Optional) See instructions page 1.			
I	Special prayer for revival during a.m. and p.m. worship services. (See instructions on page 1.) STEERING COMMITTEE MEETING: Be prepared to give progress report.			In-Church Cottage Prayer Mtgs. during midweek service. (See instructions page 1.)			
REVIVAL							

Fill in revival dates then back up and fill in the other dates on the calendar. You will have a tailor-made countdown calendar for your committee.

Prayer Commitment Card

for Revival _____ (dates)

_____ Yes, I will pray daily for our revival. I will set aside a time each day at approximately _____ (time of day).

_____ Yes, my family and I will pray for our revival daily.

Signed _____

Church Revival

Remember to Pray Daily for Our

_____ (dates)

Please put this card in a place to remind you to pray for our revival.

(Fill in the dates and names in blanks and reproduce.)

Remember to Pray for Revival

Fold along dotted line and set up on meal table

evangelist _____   singer _____

_____ dates

Family Prayer for Revival

Family Prayer for Revival

_____ dates

evangelist _____   singer _____

Remember to Pray for Revival

Fold along dotted line and set up on meal table

1. Keep one copy in the book.
2. Give one copy to chairmen.

Planning for Revival

Publicity Chairman

This committee is responsible for communicating the news of the coming revival to the church membership and community

HOW TO REPRODUCE PUBLICITY MATERIALS

On three separate pages in the book you have art work for posters, leaflets, and newspaper ads. Be sure you have these. (Check with General Chairman.) In chapter nine of the book there are two other options, "Victory in Jesus" and "Church Crusade." You might prefer to use one of the options to the one provided. If so, ask the General Chairman for the art work.

1. <u>Poster</u>. 8½"x11". The top half has the logo. The lower half has been left blank for you to add the church name, location, dates and times of services.

   If possible, enlarge the poster to 11"x14" and print in a bright, bold color. If your church has an offset press, the secretary can reproduce these for you. You might have a print shop do it. If need be, these can be reproduced on a copy machine. First have someone artistic print in the information on the lower half or use prepared lettering which can be purchased at an office supply.

2. <u>Leaflet</u>. Two 5½"x8½" on one page. The front side has the logo. The back side is for you to print your church revival information. These are to be used in three ways: (1) Visitation invitations, (2) door-to-door distribution, and (3) as inserts in the church bulletin on Sunday. Reproduce these in the same manner as the poster, then cut them in two.

3. <u>Newspaper ads</u>. One and two column. Simply take these to a newspaper and give the church name and address, revival dates, and times.

SUGGESTIONS ON QUANTITIES NEEDED

1. Posters: Total needed _____

   _____ Enough to put up in department and classrooms through out the church building and on bulletin boards in hallways.

   _____ Enough to put up in store windows and schools in the community.

2. Leaflets: Total needed _____

   _____ A number equal to your average attendance for visitation purposes. (Give to visitation chairman.)

   _____ Enough to pass out door-to-door if you do this.

   _____ Twice the number of bulletins printed for Sunday worship services. (Give these to the church secretary.)

   _____ Extra copies for members to give to neighbors and friends.

Publicity Chairman Countdown Calendar

Week	Sunday	Monday	Tuesday	Wednesday	Thursday	Friday	Saturday
VI		Enlist committee if you plan to use one. Be sure you have the art work for publicity materials (see front page.)					
V		Write to the revival preacher and singer. Request biographical data and black and white glossy pictures for publicity. You might want to ask someone artistic to paint a large sign (3'x5') for the church yard. Ask someone to build the frame work and put it up on Saturday of Week II.					
IV	Ask the children's workers to be responsible for getting boys and girls to distribute circulars door-to-door on Saturday before the revival week.	Prepare and print publicity materials. (See instructions for reproducing on front page.)					
III	STEERING COMMITTEE MEETING: Be prepared to give progress report.					Put posters up in church building.	
II	STEERING COMMITTEE MEETING: Be prepared to give progress report.	Put article in the church newsletter featuring the revival music director. Include pictures. Promote revival events.				Put posters up in store windows around town and in schools. Put large sign up in church yard.	
I	Use bulletin inserts (leaflet). Make final arrangements to distribute circulars on Saturday. STEERING COMMITTEE MEETING: Be prepared to give progress report.	Put an article in church newsletter featuring the revival preacher. Include picture. Promote revival events. Take a news release article to the newspaper telling about your revival. Consider a paid ad.					Distribute circulars door-to-door.
REVIVAL	Put revival schedule on revival bulletin inserts (leaflet).						

Fill in revival dates then back up and fill in the other dates on the calendar. You will have a tailor-made countdown calendar for your committee.

Planning for Revival

1. Keep one copy in the book.
2. Give one copy to chairmen.

Publicity Chairman

This committee is responsible for communicating the news of the coming revival to the church membership and community

HOW TO REPRODUCE PUBLICITY MATERIALS

On three separate pages in the book you have art work for posters, leaflets, and newspaper ads. Be sure you have these. (Check with General Chairman.) In chapter nine of the book there are two other options, "Victory in Jesus" and "Church Crusade." You might prefer to use one of the options to the one provided. If so, ask the General Chairman for the art work.

1. <u>Poster</u>. 8½"x11". The top half has the logo. The lower half has been left blank for you to add the church name, location, dates and times of services.

    If possible, enlarge the poster to 11"x14" and print in a bright, bold color. If your church has an offset press, the secretary can reproduce these for you. You might have a print shop do it. If need be, these can be reproduced on a copy machine. First have someone artistic print in the information on the lower half or use prepared lettering which can be purchased at an office supply.

2. <u>Leaflet</u>. Two 5½"x8½" on one page. The front side has the logo. The back side is for you to print your church revival information. These are to be used in three ways: (1) Visitation invitations, (2) door-to-door distribution, and (3) as inserts in the church bulletin on Sunday. Reproduce these in the same manner as the poster, then cut them in two.

3. <u>Newspaper ads</u>. One and two column. Simply take these to a newspaper and give the church name and address, revival dates, and times.

SUGGESTIONS ON QUANTITIES NEEDED

1. Posters: Total needed _____

    _____ Enough to put up in department and classrooms through out the church building and on bulletin boards in hallways.

    _____ Enough to put up in store windows and schools in the community.

2. Leaflets: Total needed _____

    _____ A number equal to your average attendance for visitation purposes. (Give to visitation chairman.)

    _____ Enough to pass out door-to-door if you do this.

    _____ Twice the number of bulletins printed for Sunday worship services. (Give these to the church secretary.)

    _____ Extra copies for members to give to neighbors and friends.

Publicity Chairman Countdown Calendar

Week	Sunday	Monday	Tuesday	Wednesday	Thursday	Friday	Saturday
VI		Enlist committee if you plan to use one. Be sure you have the art work for publicity materials (see front page.)					
V		Write to the revival preacher and singer. Request biographical data and black and white glossy pictures for publicity. You might want to ask someone artistic to paint a large sign (3'x5') for the church yard. Ask someone to build the frame work and put it up on Saturday of Week II.					
IV		Prepare and print publicity materials. (See instructions for reproducing on front page.) Ask the children's workers to be responsible for getting boys and girls to distribute circulars door-to-door on Saturday before the revival week.					
III	STEERING COMMITTEE MEETING: Be prepared to give progress report.					Put posters up in church building.	
II	STEERING COMMITTEE MEETING: Be prepared to give progress report.	Put article in the church newsletter featuring the revival music director. Include pictures. Promote revival events.				Put posters up in store windows around town and in schools. Put large sign up in church yard.	
I	Use bulletin inserts (leaflet). Make final arrangements to distribute circulars on Saturday. STEERING COMMITTEE MEETING: Be prepared to give progress report.	Put an article in church newsletter featuring the revival preacher. Include picture. Promote revival events. Take a news release article to the newspaper telling about your revival. Consider a paid ad.					Distribute circulars door-to-door.
REVIVAL	Put revival schedule on revival bulletin inserts (leaflet).						

Fill in revival dates then back up and fill in the other dates on the calendar. You will have a tailor-made countdown calendar for your committee.

REVIVAL
Believe & Belong
Believe in Jesus
Belong to His Church

_____
(Church)

_____
(dates)

_____
(time)

Singer

[(picture)]

_____
(name)

Preacher

[(picture)]

_____
(name)

REVIVAL
Believe & Belong
Believe in Jesus
Belong to His Church

_____
(Church)

_____
(dates)

_____
(time)

Singer

[(picture)]

_____
(name)

Preacher

[(picture)]

_____
(name)

Ads for Newspaper and Church Newsletter

Simply deliver the ads to the newspaper accompanied with church information. They will add the print. For church newsletters that use offset, simply add the information yourself.

1. Keep one copy in the book.
2. Give one copy to chairmen.

Planning for Revival

Revival Secretary

1. Serve on the Steering Committee. Keep records. Contact the chairmen before each Steering Committee Meeting and remind them to please be present.

2. Keep the revival dates before members. Every newsletter and Sunday bulletin starting six weeks before the revival ought to have something about the revival and/or preparation. On separate pages in the manual you have two pages of headlines and logos. Be sure you have these. (Check with the General Chairman.)

3. Help the various committee chairmen to reproduce and order the materials they need. <u>The committees are to stuff, stamp, address and mail their own letters.</u> This is a must or the secretary will <u>be overloaded.</u> Many of the materials to be reproduced need only to fill in the blanks and make copies. This can be done on a copy machine or by offset press. Many quick print shops can make copies fairly inexpensively. Churches without copy machines can get copies made at some business, school, another church, post office, etc. You might have electronic stencils made or cut your own stencils and mimeograph. Ask each chairman to get the materials to be reproduced to you early so you can keep ahead of schedule. <u>When they delay, it is your job to remind them that materials need to be prepared.</u>

In smaller churches where there is no paid secretary, the pastor will need to enlist a lady (or ladies) who can type. In some cases, the chairmen may need to get their own materials reproduced. The pastor needs to help with this.

In larger churches where there are several secretaries, the work may be divided among them, but the Revival Secretary has the responsibility to see that the work is done.

Revival Secretary Countdown Calendar

Week	Sunday	Monday	Tuesday	Wednesday	Thursday	Friday	Saturday
VI							
V			Help Prayer Chairman reproduce materials. Reproduce "I Know A Prospect" cards for Visitation Chairman. Put article in newsletter about revival dates, Steering Committee, etc.				
IV			Help Music Chairman prepare choir enlistment cards and memo. Help Publicity Chairman prepare and print materials. Help Sunday School Chairman reproduce materials.			Call Steering Committee members about meeting Sunday.	
III	STEERING COMMITTEE MEETING #1		Help Youth Chairman reproduce memo and tickets. Reproduce letters from pastor to prospects and from evangelist to members. (See pastor.) Put prayer reminder in church mailout and Sunday bulletin. (Check with Prayer Chm.)			Call Steering Committee members about meet- Sunday.	
II	STEERING COMMITTEE MEETING #2		Help Adult Chairman reproduce memo. Help Children's Chairman reproduce memo and tickets. Help Contact Chairman reproduce memo and invitation cards. Put article in church mailout about singer for revival. (Check with Publicity Chm.)			Call Steering Committee about meeting.	
I	Put an insert in bulletin with revival information. STEERING COMMITTEE MEETING #3		Mail letters from pastor to prospects and from evangelist to members. Enlist some ladies to help stuff, stamp, and address letters. Put article in church mailout about revival preacher. Promote revival events. (Check with Publicity Chm.)				
REVIVAL	Put an insert in bulletin with revival schedule.						

Fill in revival dates then back up and fill in the other dates on the calendar. You will have a tailor-made countdown calendar for your committee.

1. Keep one copy in the book.
2. Give one copy to chairmen.

Planning for Revival

Revival Secretary

1. Serve on the Steering Committee. Keep records. Contact the chairmen before each Steering Committee Meeting and remind them to please be present.

2. Keep the revival dates before members. Every newsletter and Sunday bulletin starting six weeks before the revival ought to have something about the revival and/or preparation. On separate pages in the manual you have two pages of headlines and logos. Be sure you have these. (Check with the General Chairman.)

3. Help the various committee chairmen to reproduce and order the materials they need. <u>The committees are to stuff, stamp, address and mail their own letters.</u> This is a must or the secretary will <u>be overloaded.</u> Many of the materials to be reproduced need only to fill in the blanks and make copies. This can be done on a copy machine or by offset press. Many quick print shops can make copies fairly inexpensively. Churches without copy machines can get copies made at some business, school, another church, post office, etc. You might have electronic stencils made or cut your own stencils and mimeograph. Ask each chairman to get the materials to be reproduced to you early so you can keep ahead of schedule. <u>When they delay, it is your job to remind them that materials need to be prepared.</u>

In smaller churches where there is no paid secretary, the pastor will need to enlist a lady (or ladies) who can type. In some cases, the chairmen may need to get their own materials reproduced. The pastor needs to help with this.

In larger churches where there are several secretaries, the work may be divided among them, but the Revival Secretary has the responsibility to see that the work is done.

Revival Secretary Countdown Calendar

Week	Sunday	Monday	Tuesday	Wednesday	Thursday	Friday	Saturday
VI							
V			Help Prayer Chairman reproduce materials. Reproduce "I Know A Prospect" cards for Visitation Chairman. Put article in newsletter about revival dates, Steering Committee, etc.				
IV			Help Music Chairman prepare choir enlistment cards and memo. Help Publicity Chairman prepare and print materials. Help Sunday School Chairman reproduce materials.			Call Steering Committee members about meeting Sunday.	
III	STEERING COMMITTEE MEETING #1		Help Youth Chairman reproduce memo and tickets. Reproduce letters from pastor to prospects and from evangelist to members. (See pastor.) Put prayer reminder in church mailout and Sunday bulletin. (Check with Prayer Chm.)			Call Steering Committee members about meet- Sunday.	
II	STEERING COMMITTEE MEETING #2		Help Adult Chairman reproduce memo. Help Children's Chairman reproduce memo and tickets. Help Contact Chairman reproduce memo and invitation cards. Put article in church mailout about singer for revival. (Check with Publicity Chm.)			Call Steering Committee about meeting.	
I	Put an insert in bulletin with revival information. STEERING COMMITTEE MEETING #3		Mail letters from pastor to prospects and from evangelist to members. Enlist some ladies to help stuff, stamp, and address letters. Put article in church mailout about revival preacher. Promote revival events. (Check with Publicity Chm.)				
REVIVAL	Put an insert in bulletin with revival schedule.						

Fill in revival dates then back up and fill in the other dates on the calendar. You will have a tailor-made countdown calendar for your committee.

Men and Women's Night at the Revival
Sunday School Rally Night   Family Night at the Revival
Bring The Family to Family Night, Friday   Youth Joy Explosion
Children's Corny Dog Supper   Believe & Belong Revival
Youth C.I.F. Fellowship   Pray for Revival   Revival Schedule
Pray for Believe & Belong Revival   Believe & Belong
Attend our Believe & Belong Revival   Revival Visitation

Youth C.I.F. Fellowship   Pray for Revival

Attend our Believe & Belong Revival

Pray for Believe & Belong Revival

Men and Women's Night at the Revival

Sunday School Rally Night   Pray for Revival

Believe & Belong Revival

Bring The Family to Family Night, Friday

Children's Corny Dog Supper

Believe & Belong   Youth Joy Explosion

Family Night at the Revival   Family Night

Revival Schedule   Revival Visitation

Attend our Believe & Belong Revival

Pray for Believe & Belong Revival

Believe & Belong Revival   Revival Visitation

Revival Schedule   Believe & Belong

1. Keep one copy in the book.
2. Give one copy to chairmen.

Planning for Revival

Sunday School Chairman

The Sunday School Director should probably be chairman of this committee. His committee will be the Sunday School Council (teachers in smaller churches; department directors or division coordinators in larger churches).

I. UNITED EVANGELISTIC SERVICE

This is to be held on the first Sunday morning of the revival unless the evangelist is present for the last Sunday morning only. This is for grades four to twelve, but other ages might be included. Meet in regular class areas first, fill out records and go to auditorium.

The evangelist will teach everyone present how to be saved and know it. (Ask the pastor to communicate this to the evangelist.) Teachers should be prepared to counsel those who make decisions when the invitation is offered.

II. SUNDAY SCHOOL RALLY NIGHT ON MONDAY EVENING OF THE REVIVAL

This is a Sunday School emphasis with the departments and/or classes seeking to have at least their average attendance present on Monday evening of the revival. <u>This is an extremely important event</u>.

It assures a good attendance on the first week night revival service. It puts the biggest and best organization in the church working to build a good attendance on the hardest night to get a good crowd present. <u>This plan works great if you will work hard at it.</u> It can be fun and effective. Here is how it works:

1. On the Sunday before the revival week promote Sunday School Rally Night in departments and classes. Begin signing up class and department members who will commit themselves to be present for Sunday School Rally Night on Monday of the revival week. Plan to have as many members present on Monday evening as you average in Sunday School.

2. On the first Sunday of the revival complete signing up department and class members to be present on Sunday School Rally Night, Monday night. That afternoon teachers and/or directors call those not yet signed up.

3. On Monday evening each department/class fills up their section of the building. A banner with each department or class name on it indicates the seating space. Departments or classes will be recognized in the service so each should work hard to have a large group present. You might choose not to sit together and eliminate banners.

III. SATURDAY, VISITATION TO THOSE WHO MADE DECISIONS

Prior to Saturday the director sees that each teacher has the name of those who are prospects for his class who made decisions during the revival week. The teacher is to visit (or call) each of these and invite them to be in Sunday School the next morning. Let's get them started off right by getting them enrolled in Sunday School.

Instructions for Reproducing Sign-up Cards

On a separate page in the manual you have "Sunday School Rally Night" sign-up cards. Be sure to secure these. (Check with General Chairman.)

To reproduce the cards fill in revival dates, make copies, and cut apart. These need to be on card stock if possible. Ask the Revival Secretary to help reproduce these. They will be used for sign-up on Sundays of Weeks II and I.

If there is no Revival Secretary, then you might have a quick print shop reproduce these for you. Or you might have copies made on a copy machine. Many businesses like banks, or schools, or other churches have copy machines and will help with this. <u>Ask your pastor to help with this.</u>

Sunday School Chairman Countdown Calendar

Week	Sunday	Monday	Tuesday	Wednesday	Thursday	Friday	Saturday
VI							
V							
IV				Make copies of instructions on front page to give to each teacher and department director. Call a meeting of all teachers and department directors for next Wednesday (Week II) at which time you will give them this piece of material and explain it. Ask the secretary to help reproduce the material or make xerox copies. Also, prepare sign-up cards (see instructions on front page).			
III	STEERING COMMITTEE MEETING: Be prepared to give progress report.						
II	Remind teachers and directors of the meeting Wednesday. Pray for Revival in Sunday school classes/departments. STEERING COMMITTEE MEETING: Be prepared to give report.		Have someone call directors who, in turn, call teachers reminding them to meet Wednesday.	Meet with S.S. teachers and officers and explain events. Distribute material prepared earlier.			
I	Pray for revival in S.S. and promote S.S. Rally Night on Monday of revival in all S.S. departments. Teachers/directors begin signing up class/dept. members who will commit themselves to be present. STEERING COMMITTEE MEETING		Prepare banners to be used to designate sections of the auditorium for classes or departments. (See sample on back of page with sign-up cards.) Enlist and train teachers to counsel with those who will make decisions at the United Evangelistic Service during Sunday School.				
REVIVAL	UNITED EVANGELISTIC SERVICE Teachers and officers continue signing up all of class/department members to be present on S.S. Rally Night tomorrow evening. This afternoon teachers call those not yet signed up and enlist them to be present.	Put up banners designating sections of building for classes/departments. S.S. RALLY NIGHT	Early in the service on Monday evening ask the pastor to recognize classes/departments. You may or may not want to take a count and award the class/department with the largest attendance or percentage. Then remove the banners and have small children go sit with parents. This all should take no more than 5 to 8 minutes.				Visits to new members. (See III on front page.)

Fill in revival dates then back up and fill in the other dates on the calendar. You will have a tailor-made countdown calendar for your committee.

1. Keep one copy in the book.
2. Give one copy to chairmen.

Planning for Revival

Sunday School Chairman

The Sunday School Director should probably be chairman of this committee. His committee will be the Sunday School Council (teachers in smaller churches; department directors or division coordinators in larger churches).

I. UNITED EVANGELISTIC SERVICE

This is to be held on the first Sunday morning of the revival unless the evangelist is present for the last Sunday morning only. This is for grades four to twelve, but other ages might be included. Meet in regular class areas first, fill out records and go to auditorium.

The evangelist will teach everyone present how to be saved and know it. (Ask the pastor to communicate this to the evangelist.) Teachers should be prepared to counsel those who make decisions when the invitation is offered.

II. SUNDAY SCHOOL RALLY NIGHT ON MONDAY EVENING OF THE REVIVAL

This is a Sunday School emphasis with the departments and/or classes seeking to have at least their average attendance present on Monday evening of the revival. <u>This is an extremely important event.</u>

It assures a good attendance on the first week night revival service. It puts the biggest and best organization in the church working to build a good attendance on the hardest night to get a good crowd present. <u>This plan works great if you will work hard at it</u>. It can be fun and effective. Here is how it works:

1. On the Sunday before the revival week promote Sunday School Rally Night in departments and classes. Begin signing up class and department members who will commit themselves to be present for Sunday School Rally Night on Monday of the revival week. Plan to have as many members present on Monday evening as you average in Sunday School.

2. On the first Sunday of the revival complete signing up department and class members to be present on Sunday School Rally Night, Monday night. That afternoon teachers and/or directors call those not yet signed up.

3. On Monday evening each department/class fills up their section of the building. A banner with each department or class name on it indicates the seating space. Departments or classes will be recognized in the service so each should work hard to have a large group present. You might choose not to sit together and eliminate banners.

III. SATURDAY, VISITATION TO THOSE WHO MADE DECISIONS

Prior to Saturday the director sees that each teacher has the name of those who are prospects for his class who made decisions during the revival week. The teacher is to visit (or call) each of these and invite them to be in Sunday School the next morning. Let's get them started off right by getting them enrolled in Sunday School.

Instructions for Reproducing Sign-up Cards

On a separate page in the manual you have "Sunday School Rally Night" sign-up cards. Be sure to secure these. (Check with General Chairman.)

To reproduce the cards fill in revival dates, make copies, and cut apart. These need to be on card stock if possible. Ask the Revival Secretary to help reproduce these. They will be used for sign-up on Sundays of Weeks II and I.

If there is no Revival Secretary, then you might have a quick print shop reproduce these for you. Or you might have copies made on a copy machine. Many businesses like banks, or schools, or other churches have copy machines and will help with this. <u>Ask your pastor to help with this.</u>

Sunday School Chairman Countdown Calendar

Week	Sunday	Monday	Tuesday	Wednesday	Thursday	Friday	Saturday
VI							
V							
IV		Make copies of instructions on front page to give to each teacher and department director. Call a meeting of all teachers and department directors for next Wednesday (Week II) at which time you will give them this piece of material and explain it. Ask the secretary to help reproduce the material or make xerox copies. Also, prepare sign-up cards (see instructions on front page).					
III	STEERING COMMITTEE MEETING: Be prepared to give progress report.						
II	Remind teachers and directors of the meeting Wednesday. Pray for Revival in Sunday school classes/departments. STEERING COMMITTEE MEETING: Be prepared to give report.		Have someone call directors who, in turn, call teachers reminding them to meet Wednesday.	Meet with S.S. teachers and officers and explain events. Distribute material prepared earlier.			
I	Pray for revival in S.S. and promote S.S. Rally Night on Monday of revival in all S.S. departments. Teachers/directors begin signing up class/dept. members who will commit themselves to be present. STEERING COMMITTEE MEETING		Prepare banners to be used to designate sections of the auditorium for classes or departments. (See sample on back of page with sign-up cards.) Enlist and train teachers to counsel with those who will make decisions at the United Evangelistic Service during Sunday School.				
REVIVAL	UNITED EVANGELISTIC SERVICE Teachers and officers continue signing up all of class/department members to be present on S.S. Rally Night tomorrow evening. This afternoon teachers call those not yet signed up and enlist them to be present.	Put up banners designating sections of building for classes/departments. S.S. RALLY NIGHT	Early in the service on Monday evening ask the pastor to recognize classes/departments. You may or may not want to take a count and award the class/department with the largest attendance or percentage. Then <u>remove the banners</u> and have small children go sit with parents. This all should take no more than 5 to 8 minutes.				Visits to new members. (See III on front page.)

Fill in revival dates then back up and fill in the other dates on the calendar. You will have a tailor-made countdown calendar for your committee.

Sunday School Rally Night at the Revival on Monday

(Revival Dates)

___ Yes, I will attend the Monday evening revival service to help represent my department/class in a big way.

Signed ___

Sunday School Rally Night at the Revival on Monday

(Revival Dates)

___ Yes, I will attend the Monday evening revival service to help represent my department/class in a big way.

Signed ___

Sunday School Rally Night at the Revival on Monday

(Revival Dates)

___ Yes, I will attend the Monday evening revival service to help represent my department/class in a big way.

Signed ___

Sunday School Rally Night at the Revival on Monday

(Revival Dates)

___ Yes, I will attend the Monday evening revival service to help represent my department/class in a big way.

Signed ___

BANNER

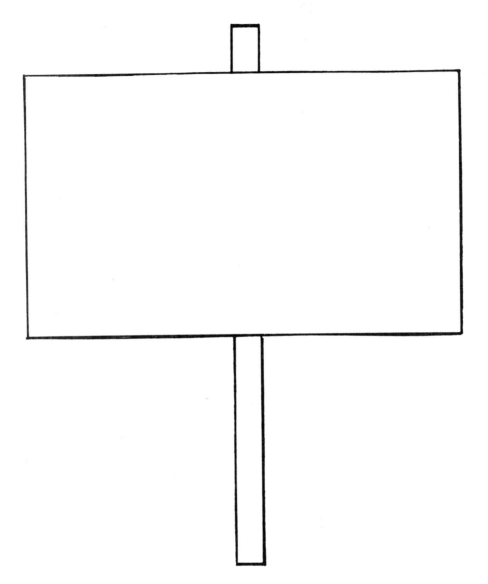

Cut a poster board in half and staple it back to back with ½"x1" stake stapled in between for the handle. Print the name of the department or class in large letters. Prior to the Monday evening service use masking tape to tape banners to pews. You might prefer another way to do this. The primary purpose of the banner is to indicate the sections reserved for each department or class.

1. Keep one copy in the book.
2. Give one copy to chairmen.

Planning for Revival

Visitation Chairman

This committee is responsible for pre-revival visitation. Two weeks before the revival we will concentrate on visiting less active church members. One week before the revival we will visit unsaved and unchurched prospects. Set a goal to have 20 people visiting for the revival for every 100 you average in Sunday School or church attendance.

LOCATE PROSPECTS FOR VISITATION

This is imperative for successful revival visitation. Three methods are suggested although others may be used to do whatever is necessary to locate prospects. Make this a committee project.

1. <u>Update the prospect file</u>. Eliminate the names of those who have moved, joined other churches, etc. Add the names of newcomers to the community, recent church visitors, etc. Prepare the file for use.
2. <u>Examination of Sunday School and church rolls</u>. Determine unsaved and unchurched from Sunday School and church membership rolls. Consider as prospects family members of those enrolled.
3. <u>Inside Survey</u>. Take an inside survey during Sunday School (or worship service) on the Sunday of Weeks IV and III. Department/class outreach leaders can help with this. Give every adult-youth in Sunday School one or more "I Know A Prospect" card. Ask them to write the names of relatives, fellow workers, classmates, neighbors, friends, etc. who are unsaved or unchurched. Work out the details ahead of time. Be prepared to process these into the prospect file.

SCHEDULING VISITATION

Tuesday evening and Saturday morning are suggested for revival visitation. You may prefer a different night or Sunday. Choose the best two times for you and encourage visitors to participate both days each week.

Meet Tuesday evening at 7:00 for assignments. Plan a report session at 8:30, 8:45, or 9:00. Report on visits and turn in assignment cards. You may plan a soup and sandwich supper before visitation and/or light refreshments for the report session.

On Saturday morning, meet at 10:00 for assignments and report at noon. Perhaps, you could have a brunch or light lunch.

Provide child care during visitation. Make alterations as best fits your situation.

MAKING ASSIGNMENTS

Have an envelope for each person enlisted to visit with his name (or couple's name) on it. Put three assignments in it ahead of time (six for couples). They simply pick up their envelope of assignments and go visiting. When they return from visiting, take up the envelopes. Prior to Saturday's visitation, remove cards of those visited and replace them with new assignments. Do this both weeks.

You may prefer to have assignment envelopes without names on them and three assignment cards in each, grouped by location. Each person visiting would pick up an envelope. (Husbands and wives would each get one envelope.)

Or you may prefer to have assignment cards put on tables for people to choose whom they want to visit. You might have tables set up and cards set out by Sunday School departments. <u>Please be aware that this takes a lot of time and is not nearly as effective.</u>

On the night of visitation, pair up people to visit. Husbands and wives should go together. Then pair up those who need a partner. Each person will have three assignments or six assignments together. They need this many to be sure to contact at least three families/persons.

Give the pastor the cards of those who have been visited with comments about the visits.

NOTE: On a separate page in the manual you have art work for "I Know A Prospect" cards. On the back is a copy of the sample letter suggested in the instructions. Be sure you have this. (Check with General Chairman.)

Visitation Chairman Countdown Calendar

Week	Sunday	Monday	Tuesday	Wednesday	Thursday	Friday	Saturday
VI	Enlist committee. Enlist someone from each Sunday School department/class. Share plans with them. Work with pastor to: (1) Prepare a list of people you want to ask to visit for the revival. Include Sunday School teachers and officers, deacons, etc., and anyone who might visit, including youth. (2) Begin plans to locate prospects; (3) Prepare letter to each person you want to enlist for revival visitation. (See instructions on front page.) Ask the secretary to reproduce the letter, but your committee is to stuff, stamp, and address it. Mail next week.						
V	Ask the secretary to reproduce the "I Know A Prospect" cards. (See instructions on front page.)	Mail letter					
IV	Conduct inside survey (see instructions). Enlist visitors for special revival visitation. You and your committee call all those to whom letters were sent and get their commitment to participate in revival visitation. You might begin the conversation like this: "I am calling in behalf of the pastor to find out if you plan to participate with us in visitation for our upcoming church revival."						
III	Conclude Inside Survey. STEERING COMMITTEE MEETING: Be prepared to give progress report.	Prepare visitation assignment cards. You are going to need at least three less active families for each person to visit two weeks before the revival (6 for couples). To get these, start with the most inactive and move upward toward more active until you have enough less active families to visit. You are going to need at least three prospects (families or individuals) for each person to visit the week before the revival. Enlist lots of help to get this done. Larger churches may need to start earlier.					
II	Promote visitation in Sunday School departments/classes. STEERING COMMITTEE MEETING: Be prepared to give progress report.	Ask the secretary to announce revival visitation in the Sunday bulletin and weekly mailout.	Visitation to less active members.				Visitation to less active members.
I	Promote visitation in Sunday School departments/classes. STEERING COMMITTEE MEETING: Be prepared to give progress report.		Visitation to prospects				Visitation to prospects
REVIVAL	Participants in the special revival visitation should be encouraged to bring those they visited to the revival services. Most people who make decisions in revival services are brought by someone so let's encourage them. Ask the pastor to recognize those who participated in revival visitation on Sunday evening during the service.						

Fill in revival dates then back up and fill in the other dates on the calendar. You will have a tailor-made countdown calendar for your committee.

Notes in top right:
1. Keep one copy in the book.
2. Give one copy to chairmen.

I Know a Prospect

Name _____

Address _____

Phone number _____

Approximate Age _____ Christian: Yes ___ No ___

Church Member: Yes ___ No ___
Additional information about the prospect or his family _____

_____

_____

Sign your name _____

I Know a Prospect

Name _____

Address _____

Phone number _____

Approximate Age _____ Christian: Yes ___ No ___

Church Member: Yes ___ No ___
Additional information about the prospect or his family _____

_____

_____

Sign your name _____

I Know a Prospect

Name _____

Address _____

Phone number _____

Approximate Age _____ Christian: Yes ___ No ___

Church Member: Yes ___ No ___
Additional information about the prospect or his family _____

_____

_____

Sign your name _____

I Know a Prospect

Name _____

Address _____

Phone number _____

Approximate Age _____ Christian: Yes ___ No ___

Church Member: Yes ___ No ___
Additional information about the prospect or his family _____

_____

_____

Sign your name _____

SAMPLE LETTER

Letter from Outreach Chairman and pastor to those you hope to enlist for revival visitation. Make the letter as personal as you can.

Dear _____:

I am asking you to participate in the special visitation plans for our coming revival, _____(dates).

There will be two special weeks of personal visitation. Two weeks before the revival week we will visit less active members, and the week before the revival we will visit prospective families. We will visit on Tuesday evening and Saturday morning.

The purpose of these visits is to help prepare our membership for revival and reach the unchurched and unsaved folk in our community.

In the next few days, you will be receiving a telephone call for your answer. Please pray about this matter and be prepared to tell us you will participate in revival visitation.

May God bless and help us as we seek to reach our community for Jesus Christ.

Sincerely yours,

_____
Pastor

_____
Outreach Chairman

Instructions for Reproducing "I Know A Prospect" Cards

Reproduce on card stock if possible. Then cut the cards apart. Ask the Revival Secretary to help with this.

If there is no Revival Secretary, you might reproduce these at a quick print shop. Or you might have copies made on a copy machine. Many businesses like banks, schools, or other churches have copy machines and will help you. You might just use index cards and have people write the names of prospects.

1. Keep one copy in the book.
2. Give one copy to chairmen.

Planning for Revival

Youth Chairman

This committee is responsible for the youth events in preparation for revival.

1. Youth Joy Explosion one hour before the Tuesday evening service. This is a good way to build a good attendance early in the revival week which is very important. If youth get behind the revival early, they will greatly add to a good revival attendance all week.

For the special feature you might want to have a pizza supper. If so, keep the menu simple, pizza and cold drinks. You might prefer to have spaghetti, hamburgers, tacos, banana splits, but be aware that these often take too much time to serve. The eating part should not take more than 20 minutes. Take about 15 minutes for fun time or use a popular guest personality to share a testimony. Leave about 10 minutes for the evangelist to share the plan of salvation. Don't have a sermon at this time.

Register everyone present by having them put the following information on a 3"x5" index card: name, address, telephone number, where they go to church, and how often. Provide pencils. New prospects should be discovered from the information given.

Do not call this evening "Youth Night." This might cause some adults to miss the service.

2. Youth C.I.F. Fellowship on Friday evening following the revival service. "C.I.F." stands for "Christianity Is Fun", so plan a good enjoyable fellowship for your youth. Serve light refreshments.

3. A Youth Phone Crew will be enlisted to call all the youth twice during the revival week.

4. Work with the revival Sunday School Chairman to promote the Sunday School Rally Night on Monday evening of the revival week. Be sure the youth are well represented.

Plan carefully and thoroughly to make the youth participation in the revival most enjoyable and inspiring. Work hard to get unsaved, unchurched, and inactive youth to attend the revival services. Many will make important, life changing decisions for Christ.

Instructions for Reproducing Memo and Tickets

On a separate page in the manual, you have two pieces of art work, "Youth Memo!" and "Youth Joy Explosion" tickets. Be sure you have this. (Check with the General Chairman.)

To prepare the memo, you need only to type a note in the center of the page to the youth about the Youth Joy Explosion and C.I.F. fellowship. Make it sound exciting. Fill in the needed information at the bottom of the memo. To prepare the tickets, fill in the blanks, reproduce, and cut apart. If you have a pizza supper put that on the ticket as your special feature. If you use a popular guest personality, put his/her name as the special feature, etc.

If there is no Revival Secretary, then type or handwrite the information. To reproduce these you might take them to a quick print shop. Or you might have copies made on a copy machine. Many businesses like banks, schools, or other churches have copy machines and will help with this. One way or another, you can do it. Ask the pastor to help with this.

Be sure to put the time the Youth Joy Explosion begins and also time revival service ends. Example: 6:30-8:45. If you don't put both times, many youth may go home after the Joy Explosion and not stay for the revival service.

Youth Chairman Countdown Calendar

Week	Sunday	Monday	Tuesday	Wednesday	Thursday	Friday	Saturday
VI	Enlist committee which should include workers with youth and perhaps some of the young people themselves.						
V	Enlist ladies to be responsible for meal and/or refreshments. If you serve pizza, then these ladies should enlist mothers to make or buy pizza and bring them to the church Tuesday evening hot and ready to serve. Have an oven or roster or microwave oven to keep pizzas hot. Remind the ladies that the eating should take no more than 20 minutes so use several serving lines and have things ready to pick up.						
IV	Enlist youth to serve on the Youth Phone Crew. Plan to call all the youth who are members or prospects two times. You need two young people for every 15 youth to be called. Half of them will make #1 telephone calls on Sunday and Monday of the revival week to advertise the revival and remind youth to attend the Joy Explosion on Tuesday evening. The other half will make the #2 calls on Wednesday and Thursday to advertise the revival and Youth C.I.F. Fellowship on Friday after the service. Call after school.						
III	STEERING COMMITTEE MEETING: Be prepared to give progress report.	Ask the secretary to reproduce the memo and tickets (see instructions on front page). You will need five tickets to send in each letter and extras to hand out on Sunday when the revival begins. Don't send brother's and sister's letters together. Each gets his own letter and tickets.					
II	Ask youth to make posters to advertise youth events during revival. STEERING COMMITTEE MEETING: Be prepared to give progress report.	Prepare assignment lists of young people for the Youth Phone Crew to call. Remember each crew calls all the youth so that the young people get two calls. Put 15 names and phone numbers on each page for crew #1 and make a copy for crew #2.					
I	STEERING COMMITTEE MEETING: Be prepared to give progress report.	Address, stuff, and stamp memo and tickets and mail on Wednesday. Mail or deliver telephone assignments to Youth Telephone Crews.					
REVIVAL	During Sunday School promote youth events during revival. Give out extra tickets. Also sign up youth for Sunday School Rally Night. Youth Phone Crew	SUNDAY SCHOOL RALLY NIGHT #1 makes calls.	YOUTH JOY EXPLOSION		Youth Phone Crew #2 makes calls.	YOUTH C.I.F. FELLOWSHIP	

Fill in revival dates then back up and fill in the other dates on the calendar. You will have a tailor-made countdown calendar for your committee.

1. Keep one copy in the book.
2. Give one copy to chairmen.

Planning for Revival

Youth Chairman

This committee is responsible for the youth events in preparation for revival.

1. Youth Joy Explosion one hour before the Tuesday evening service. This is a good way to build a good attendance early in the revival week which is very important. If youth get behind the revival early, they will greatly add to a good revival attendance all week.

For the special feature you might want to have a pizza supper. If so, keep the menu simple, pizza and cold drinks. You might prefer to have spaghetti, hamburgers, tacos, banana splits, but be aware that these often take too much time to serve. The eating part should not take more than 20 minutes. Take about 15 minutes for fun time or use a popular guest personality to share a testimony. Leave about 10 minutes for the evangelist to share the plan of salvation. Don't have a sermon at this time.

Register everyone present by having them put the following information on a 3"x5" index card: name, address, telephone number, where they go to church, and how often. Provide pencils. New prospects should be discovered from the information given.

Do not call this evening "Youth Night." This might cause some adults to miss the service.

2. Youth C.I.F. Fellowship on Friday evening following the revival service. "C.I.F." stands for "Christianity Is Fun", so plan a good enjoyable fellowship for your youth. Serve light refreshments.

3. A Youth Phone Crew will be enlisted to call all the youth twice during the revival week.

4. Work with the revival Sunday School Chairman to promote the Sunday School Rally Night on Monday evening of the revival week. Be sure the youth are well represented.

Plan carefully and thoroughly to make the youth participation in the revival most enjoyable and inspiring. Work hard to get unsaved, unchurched, and inactive youth to attend the revival services. Many will make important, life changing decisions for Christ.

Instructions for Reproducing Memo and Tickets

On a separate page in the manual, you have two pieces of art work, "Youth Memo!" and "Youth Joy Explosion" tickets. Be sure you have this. (Check with the General Chairman.)

To prepare the memo, you need only to type a note in the center of the page to the youth about the Youth Joy Explosion and C.I.F. fellowship. Make it sound exciting. Fill in the needed information at the bottom of the memo. To prepare the tickets, fill in the blanks, reproduce, and cut apart. If you have a pizza supper put that on the ticket as your special feature. If you use a popular guest personality, put his/her name as the special feature, etc.

If there is no Revival Secretary, then type or handwrite the information. To reproduce these you might take them to a quick print shop. Or you might have copies made on a copy machine. Many businesses like banks, schools, or other churches have copy machines and will help with this. One way or another, you can do it. Ask the pastor to help with this.

Be sure to put the time the Youth Joy Explosion begins and also time revival service ends. Example: 6:30-8:45. If you don't put both times, many youth may go home after the Joy Explosion and not stay for the revival service.

Youth Chairman Countdown Calendar

Week	Sunday	Monday	Tuesday	Wednesday	Thursday	Friday	Saturday
VI	Enlist committee which should include workers with youth and perhaps some of the young people themselves.						
V	Enlist ladies to be responsible for meal and/or refreshments. If you serve pizza, then these ladies should enlist mothers to make or buy pizza and bring them to the church Tuesday evening hot and ready to serve. Have an oven or roster or microwave oven to keep pizzas hot. Remind the ladies that the eating should take no more than 20 minutes so use several serving lines and have things ready to pick up.						
IV	Enlist youth to serve on the Youth Phone Crew. Plan to call all the youth who are members or prospects two times. You need two young people for every 15 youth to be called. Half of them will make #1 telephone calls on Sunday and Monday of the revival week to advertise the revival and remind youth to attend the Joy Explosion on Tuesday evening. The other half will make the #2 calls on Wednesday and Thursday to advertise the revival and Youth C.I.F. Fellowship on Friday after the service. Call after school.						
III	STEERING COMMITTEE MEETING: Be prepared to give progress report.	Ask the secretary to reproduce the memo and tickets (see instructions on front page). You will need five tickets to send in each letter and extras to hand out on Sunday when the revival begins. Don't send brother's and sister's letters together. Each gets his own letter and tickets.					
II	Ask youth to make posters to advertise youth events during revival. STEERING COMMITTEE MEETING: Be prepared to give progress report.	Prepare assignment lists of young people for the Youth Phone Crew to call. Remember each crew calls all the youth so that the young people get two calls. Put 15 names and phone numbers on each page for crew #1 and make a copy for crew #2.					
I	STEERING COMMITTEE MEETING: Be prepared to give progress report.	Address, stuff, and stamp memo and tickets and mail on Wednesday. Mail or deliver telephone assignments to Youth Telephone Crews.					
REVIVAL	During Sunday School promote youth events during revival. Give out extra tickets. Also sign up youth for Sunday School Rally Night. Youth Phone Crew #1 makes calls.	SUNDAY SCHOOL RALLY NIGHT	YOUTH JOY EXPLOSION		Youth Phone Crew #2 makes calls.	YOUTH C.I.F. FELLOWSHIP	

Fill in revival dates then back up and fill in the other dates on the calendar. You will have a tailor-made countdown calendar for your committee.

Youth Memo!

POW! Youth Joy Explosion POW!
for junior and senior high youth

A good evening is planned for youth so round up your friends and come on.

_____
(church and location)

_____
(revival dates and time of services)

ADMIT TWO
Youth Joy Explosion

Date　　　　Day　　　　Time

Church

Address

Special Feature

ADMIT TWO
Youth Joy Explosion

Date　　　　Day　　　　Time

Church

Address

Special Feature

ADMIT TWO
Youth Joy Explosion

Date　　　　Day　　　　Time

Church

Address

Special Feature

ADMIT TWO
Youth Joy Explosion

Date　　　　Day　　　　Time

Church

Address

Special Feature

ADMIT TWO
Youth Joy Explosion

Date　　　　Day　　　　Time

Church

Address

Special Feature

ADMIT TWO
Youth Joy Explosion

Date　　　　Day　　　　Time

Church

Address

Special Feature